WHAT PEOPLE ARE SAYIN
COMMUNICATE TO CHAN

Jim Watkins is an effective communicator who is successful for all the right reasons: he writes and speaks to change lives. *Communicate to Change Lives* is essential for anyone who would do the same.

Bob Hostetler
Coauthor with Josh McDowell of *Don't Check Your Brains at the Door* and *Beyond Belief to Convictions*

If you want to change lives, this book will show you how to do just that. I have read Jim's books and articles. Whereas he is a very entertaining speaker and writer who can leave an audience howling with laughter, Jim never fails to make a serious point about ethics, personal discipline, religious conduct, or service to Christ whenever and wherever he communicates. Thus, this book is a text that comes from Jim's heart.

Dr. Dennis E. Hensley
Professor of English
Director of the Professional Writing Major
at Taylor University Fort Wayne

I laughed, I gulped, and I learned as I read Jim's book. As a writer, speaker, and teacher of writing, Jim knows what he is talking about. Best of all, he knows how to put the teaching at a level that we can easily grasp and apply. Here's the book that will help you to change lives.

Roger Palms
Writer, teacher, speaker
Former editor of *Decision* magazine

Communicate to Change Lives is an essential tool for crossover communicators who want to reach beyond the pews with their Christian message. The author's advice is logical, original, and is delivered with typical Watkins wit: funny, wise, and authentic. It's a rare book that entertains even as it teaches. This one does both.

Holly Miller
Senior Editor at *The Saturday Evening Post*

James Watkins is a rare talent who combines humor with keen insight on the craft of good writing and speaking. Be prepared to dog-ear this book because it contains a series of ideas that will help communicators improve and enjoy themselves in the process.

Dr. Michael Ray Smith
Author of *FeatureWriting.Net*
Professor at Campbell University

An intensely practical and occasionally hilarious book for people who want to become better communicators.

Keith Drury
Author of *Holiness for Ordinary People*
Professor at Indiana Wesleyan University

This book is a must-have for *every* writer and speaker.

Reg A. Forder
Director of American Christian Writers, ACW Press

I've been quoting Jim at my seminars for years and can highly recommend him. With wisdom and wit he challenges writers and speakers to know their message, know their audience, and know the keys to effective communication. This is a book all writers and speakers need to read more than once and refer to frequently if they are serious about changing lives.

Marlene Bagnull
Write His Answer Ministries
Director of Colorado and Greater Philadelphia
Christian Writers Conferences

COMMUNICATE TO
CHANGE LIVES
IN PERSON AND PRINT

james n. watkins

wesleyan
publishing
house

Indianapolis, Indiana

To the late Ken Taylor and his paraphrase, *The Living Bible*.
It changed my life.

CONTENTS

FOREWORD

This is a true story. I am the director of a large writing program at Taylor University Fort Wayne. A few years ago I had a terrible fall that resulted in a broken hip. Our college dean panicked. "Who can we ever get to step in with no notice to teach your classes in fiction writing, journalism, and nonfiction book writing?" he asked me. Through gritted teeth, I said, "I know of only one person. Call Jim Watkins and see if he can take over my program for a couple of weeks. Beg if you have to." Fortunately for us, Jim accepted the challenge, and he was so marvelous we later did our best to hire him full-time as a faculty member. (Odd duck that he is, he turned us down so he could continue his career as an author and national speaker. Who'd have thought, eh?)

That story brings out two aspects of the character of my longtime friend and fellow wordsmith: First, Jim is a genuine Christian brother who will do anything he can to serve the Lord by serving others; and second, he is a man who knows all the ins and outs of Christian publishing and speaking. And well he should, after three decades of experience as a magazine editor, book publishing company staff member, multi-award-winning author, conference speaker, college professor, newspaper columnist, published humorist, and literary critic.

I have listened to Jim Watkins teach many times. Additionally, I have read his books and articles. Whereas he is a very entertaining speaker and writer who can leave an audience howling with laughter, he never fails to make a serious point about ethics, personal discipline, religious conduct, or service to Christ whenever and wherever Jim communicates. Thus, this book is a text that comes from Jim's heart.

He is adamant about wanting Christians to change lives through what they speak and write, and to that end he has prepared a marvelous series of teaching and learning materials.

If writing is more than a hobby or passing fancy to you, this book is what you need. If speaking is a calling and a ministry to you, this book will show you how to fulfill your destiny. If effective communication is a joy to you and a way of expressing your love for others, then this book will give you the professional direction you've been seeking. If you want to change lives, this book will show you how to do just that.

Read this book straight through. Then set it on your writing desk within easy reach. You'll be turning back to it regularly for "refresher lessons." I know I certainly do.

DR. DENNIS E. HENSLEY
PROFESSOR OF ENGLISH
DIRECTOR OF THE PROFESSIONAL WRITING MAJOR
TAYLOR UNIVERSITY FORT WAYNE

INTRODUCTION

Most writing and speaking books for Christians are very good at teaching the techniques of writing and speaking, but I'm not aware of any that specifically deal with how to communicate to change lives. Being a Sunday school teacher, pastor, college professor, writer, board member, or conference speaker is much too hard a role to perform without feeling you're making some kind of impact on those within your sphere of influence: teaching them life-changing lessons, helping them laugh their way through a tough time, providing practical ways to live out their faith, or coming to a saving knowledge of Jesus Christ.

I believe that writing and speaking are two of the best ways to change lives.

WRITING

First, writing is personal. I won a *Campus Life* "Book of the Year" contest in which the judges were teens. One wrote, "Jim Watkins is not an author." (Ouch!) "No, it's more like he's sitting across from you at McDonald's sharing Diet Cokes." (OK, I can live with that.)

Reading is an intimate, one-to-one "conversation" between the writer and the reader. You're not sitting at a conference with a thousand others listening to a speaker, but the author is talking directly to you.

Another advantage of reading is that you set the time and place, as well as the pace. Unlike other forms of mass communication, even audio books, you can read as slowly or quickly as you like. You can easily go back and reread a section that isn't clear. And, you can high-light, underline, dog ear, and make notes in the margins of a magazine or book. (Try doing that with your iPod!)

From the writer's perspective, it is a way not only to communicate with current generations, but future generations. The New Testament implies that Apollos was a much better speaker than the apostle Paul. During the time of the famous preacher Charles Spurgeon, another pastor in London was actually considered a better preacher.

So why do we know the names of Paul and Spurgeon over Apollos and "another pastor"? They both wrote! Paul penned nearly half the New Testament and Spurgeon published his weekly sermons as well as a monthly magazine. In fact, we wouldn't have the message of God's love and redemption or the teachings of Jesus Christ if not for writing! Neither would we have the writings of Augustine, Thomas à Kempis, John Wesley, C. S. Lewis, Oswald Chambers, A. W. Tozer, or hundreds of others through the ages. Parchment, papyrus, and paper have kept the message of Christ alive and in its original, unadulterated form.

SPEAKING

But speaking has its unique advantages. Jesus never wrote a book. In fact, His only writing was scribbling in dirt (John 8:6)—and we're not even told what He wrote there. He invested His life in speaking the truth in love to relatively small groups: His inner circle of Peter, James, and John, His twelve apostles, and 120 disciples. From Wesley's small groups to Billy Graham's worldwide ministry to mil-lions of people, speaking has been used as a powerful way God has chosen to change lives.

In fact, several university studies have shown that personal commu-nication—as opposed to mass media—is most effective in changing lives. (See chapter 7.)

However, as someone who is primarily an author who speaks (rather than a speaker who writes), I strongly highlight the importance of both mediums.

CHANGED LIVES

When King Josiah found long-lost written words of God, repentance and restoration came to the Jewish nation. The letters of the apostle Paul spread Christianity throughout the known world. The Reformation was sparked by the writings of Martin Luther. Before the printing of the Gutenberg Bible, Scripture was available only to ecclesiastical elite. John Wesley's writing brought about the great revivals of England. Thomas Paine's pamphlet, *Common Sense,* was the first writing to call for independence of what would become the United States. Harriet Beecher Stowe, who wrote *Uncle Tom's Cabin*, was credited by President Abraham Lincoln as "the little lady who started the great big war" that ended slavery. Martin Luther King's "Letter from Birmingham Jail" vividly and powerfully opened the eyes of the country to the injustices of racial discrimination. In the same way, Aleksandr Solzhenitsyn's *Gulag Archipelago* exposed, to the west, the deadly oppression of Communism.

And great speeches from Peter's at Pentecost to Lincoln's Gettysburg Address to King's "I have a dream" have changed lives through the spoken word.

Writing and speaking change lives. Writing and speaking change entire cultures. Writing and speaking change eternity!

WRITING AND SPEAKING TO CHANGE LIVES

So, how do we change lives? Aristotle's *Rhetoric* is a classic study in persuasive communication. He believed it included three elements: *logos, pathos,* and *ethos.* I've dubbed them intelligence, intensity, and integrity, and have organized this book under those three categories.

Aristotle's principles are timeless and universal, working as well for politicians, pornographers, and preachers. Which brings several questions to mind:

> Can Christians ethically use the same techniques as Madison Avenue?
> Can we package Christ as we would a Chrysler?
> Is it possible to motivate without manipulating?
> Is there really any difference between Christian writing and non-Christian writing?

To answer that last question, let me turn to author Madeleine L'Engle. She was asked what makes Christian writing "Christian." Here's her answer from *Walking on Water:* "I told her that if she is truly and deeply a Christian, what she writes is going to be Christian, whether she mentions Jesus or not. And if she is not, in the most profound sense, Christian, then what she writes is not going to be Christian, no matter how many times she invokes the name of the Lord."

There may not be "sacred" or "secular" techniques for writing and speaking to change lives, but there is a uniquely Christian attitude and spirit that permeates all Christian communication. In fact, as Christians, we have the assistance of a Holy Ghostwriter: "Our gospel came to you not simply with words, but also with power, with the Holy Spirit and with deep conviction" (1 Thess. 1:5). And, there is a very large difference in the motive. We're not selling vacuum cleaners or used cars for an earthly profit. We're presenting the way, the truth, and the life of Jesus Christ that leads to eternal life. Now that's a change! That's a message worth promoting as creatively and effectively as we can.

We'll look at those questions and hopefully come to some conclusions.

And, I pray that you, too, may enjoy the sense of fulfillment and joy that you have had a part in changing lives. It is hard work, but it's worth every hour staring at a computer screen and studying a Sunday school lesson when you receive letters like these:

> I wrote to you I guess because I questioned the way I interpreted love. I feel I've been a loving person all my life until recently. Today, when I looked up "love" on the Internet and found your Web site, it did something to me. In all honesty when I saw it I said, "Oh, this is just some Bible thing; people trying to get you to believe in God." I didn't want to look at it, not because I wasn't interested, but because I am bitter. I started reading it with this attitude of sarcasm. The funny thing was, though, that for some reason I kept reading it through to the end. Even if I had thoughts of clicking out of that screen, my hand was frozen to the mouse, like God sitting me at a table saying, "Here's your lesson, now learn it!" It was very strange. Do you think God is trying to tell me something? Margo

> I finished the book [*The Why Files: Is There Really Life After Death?*] on May 23 and that evening two of my daughters were involved in an automobile accident. Sarah, 20, is home recovering; Jennifer, 19, was called home. Over the last few months, many of the parts of your book have come to mind. I have used it to minister to members of my own family.
>
> Please know you are reaching people with hope and that with His grace, we are able to serve a very loving, compassionate, and BIG God. Susie

So, whatever your venue for communicating, write and speak to change lives!

PART 1

CHANGING
LIVES WITH
INTELLIGENCE

For I want you to understand what really
matters, so that you may live pure and
blameless lives until the day of Christ's return.
Philippians 1:10 NLT

1
KNOWING
YOUR GOAL

Y ou picked up this book because you want to change lives, but exactly what do you want to change?

Do you want to give hope to depressed people? Do you want to see your readers grow in their relationship with God? Do you want your hearers to send you money?

Here are some scriptures that reveal the various motivations of the Bible's authors:

> The proverbs of Solomon son of David, king of Israel: for attaining wisdom and discipline; for understanding words of insight; for acquiring a disciplined and prudent life, doing what is right and just and fair; for giving prudence to the simple, knowledge and discretion to the young—let the wise listen and add to their learning, and let the discerning get guidance— for understanding proverbs and parables, the sayings and riddles of the wise. (Prov. 1:1–6)

> Therefore, since I myself have carefully investigated everything from the beginning, it seemed good also to me to write an orderly account for you, most excellent Theophilus, so that you may know the certainty of the things you have been taught. (Luke 1:3–4)

I appeal to you, dear brothers and sisters, by the authority of our Lord Jesus Christ, to live in harmony with each other. Let there be no divisions in the church. Rather, be of one mind, united in thought and purpose. (1 Cor. 1:10 NLT)

I am shocked that you are turning away so soon from God, who called you to himself through the loving mercy of Christ. You are following a different way that pretends to be the Good News but is not the Good News at all. You are being fooled by those who deliberately twist the truth concerning Christ. (Gal. 1:6–7 NLT)

For I want you to understand what really matters, so that you may live pure and blameless lives until the day of Christ's return. May you always be filled with the fruit of your salvation—the righteous character produced in your life by Jesus Christ—for this will bring much glory and praise to God. (Phil. 1:10–11 NLT)

We proclaim to you what we ourselves have actually seen and heard so that you may have fellowship with us. And our fellowship is with the Father and with his Son, Jesus Christ. (1 John 1:3 NLT)

THAT WAS THEN

The more specific our goal in wanting to change lives, the more powerful our communication will be. So, classical rhetoric divides persuasive messages into three categories:

Epideictic

Epideictic rhetoric seeks to praise or blame someone or something. For example, "Plagiarism is a pervasive problem in our pulpits";

"Dangerous pedophiles are looking for your children online"; "Too many doctors are overdiagnosing depression in patients."

Forensic

Forensic rhetoric seeks to prove a point. For example, "Three out of four pastors admit to using others' sermons without attribution"; "Online pedophiles sexually abuse more than 10,000 children annually"; "Last year, 150 million prescriptions were written for antidepressants." (I made up these statistics as an example, so don't quote me.)

Deliberative

Finally, deliberative rhetoric is a response to a problem. For example, "Denomination to punish pulpit plagiarism"; "Ten ways to protect your children from online predators"; and "More effective screening of possible depression needed."

THIS IS NOW

While editorial director at Wesleyan Publishing House, I was in charge of high school curriculum. Every single lesson plan had to have a cognitive, affective, and behavioral goal. At least that's what the educators on our committee called them. We simply dubbed them *Know*, *Feel*, and *Do*.

For instance, here are my goals for this book:

Cognitive goal (know): Reader will know biblical and psychological principles for writing and speaking to change lives.

Affective goal (feel): Reader will feel inspired to write material and speak in a way that will actually change lives.

Behavioral goal (do): Reader will buy this book for all his or her friends. Oops, sorry! Reader will write material and speak in a way that will actually change lives.

If we're going to change lives, our readers and listeners need to be provided an "action step." What exactly do you want your readers or class members to do? Write their legislator, give up a habit, contribute to your ministry, read a chapter of the Bible each day for a year, sign your petition, buy my book for all your writer friends?

Know exactly what you want them to know, feel, and do.

Jesus knew their thoughts.

Matthew 12:25

2

KNOWING YOUR AUDIENCE

Any fan of the TV game show *Jeopardy* can tell you that having the right answer depends on knowing the right question. And as writers and speakers who want to change lives, we need to know our audience's questions before we start blurting out answers.

G. C. Lichtenberg wrote, "The mark of a really great writer is that he gives expression to what the masses of mankind think or feel without knowing it. The mediocre writer simply writes what everyone would have said."

Jesus knew His audience's very thoughts. We don't have that ability or luxury, but as the apostle Paul modeled, we can learn what our audience is thinking:

> While Paul was . . . in Athens, he was greatly distressed to see that the city was full of idols. So he reasoned in the synagogue with the Jews and the God-fearing Greeks, as well as in the marketplace day by day with those who happened to be there. A group of Epicurean and Stoic philosophers began to dispute with him. Some of them asked, "What is this babbler trying to say?" Others remarked, "He seems to be advocating foreign gods." They said this because Paul was preaching the good

news about Jesus and the resurrection. Then they took him and brought him to a meeting of the Areopagus, where they said to him, "May we know what this new teaching is that you are presenting? You are bringing some strange ideas to our ears, and we want to know what they mean." (All the Athenians and the foreigners who lived there spent their time doing nothing but talking about and listening to the latest ideas.)

Paul then stood up in the meeting of the Areopagus and said: "Men of Athens! I see that in every way you are very religious. For as I walked around and looked carefully at your objects of worship, I even found an altar with this inscription: TO AN UNKNOWN GOD. Now what you worship as something unknown I am going to proclaim to you." (Acts 17:16–23)

Notice that Paul was in the marketplace day by day, talking with those who gathered there to discuss the latest ideas. He walked around, noting all the objects of worship, including an altar to an unknown God. He had done his market research.

Nearly half the cost of advertising production is market research. Who buys the product? Why? When? Where? How much? A successful agency knows precisely the sex, age, background, socioeconomic status, occupation, family size, politics, prejudices, struggles, needs, and frustrations of its potential buyer. Equally important is knowing the needs of the audience.

Writers and speakers who are effective in changing lives know their target market. Notice that Paul adapted his message to his audience:

Even though I am free of the demands and expectations of everyone, I have voluntarily become a servant to any and all in order to reach a wide range of people: religious, nonreligious, meticulous moralists, loose-living immoralists, the defeated, the demoralized—whoever. I didn't take on their way of life. I kept my bearings in Christ—but I entered their world and tried to experience things from their point of view. I've become just about every sort of servant there is in my attempts to lead those I meet into a God-saved life. I did all this because of the Message. I didn't just want to talk about it; I wanted to be in on it! (1 Cor. 9:20–23 MSG)

He also slanted his message to the spiritual state of his audiences: non-Christians, as well as immature and mature Christians.

When I first came to you, dear brothers and sisters, I didn't use lofty words and impressive wisdom to tell you God's secret plan. For I decided that while I was with you I would forget everything except Jesus Christ, the one who was crucified. (1 Cor. 2:1–2 NLT)

Dear brothers and sisters, when I was with you I couldn't talk to you as I would to spiritual people. I had to talk as though you belonged to this world or as though you were infants in the Christian life. I had to feed you with milk, not with solid food, because you weren't ready for anything stronger. And you still aren't ready. (1 Cor. 3:1–2 NLT)

Yet when I am among mature believers, I do speak with words of wisdom, but not the kind of wisdom that belongs to this world or to the rulers of this world, who are soon forgotten. (1 Cor. 2:6 NLT)

In his gospel, John knew his Greek audience revered words in and of themselves. So, it's no surprise he started off with "In the beginning was the Word, and the Word was with God, and the Word was God." He also knew that his readers would be familiar with the first words of Genesis.

Matthew, on the other hand, knew his Hebrew audience honored family records, so he began with the prophetic lineage of Christ: "A record of the genealogy of Jesus Christ the son of David, the son of Abraham." Both could have begun their lead sentence with the emphasis on Christ. But each passage appeals to the original readers' particular interest.

To make sure they were writing to the right audience, an evangelical denomination spent hundreds of dollars to discern its typical reader.

Mary is fifty-two, gray, wears an apron, and doesn't work outside the home. She lives in Iowa where her husband raises corn and soybeans. The sparkle is out of their marriage. Her son is in college; her daughter is in high school. She is active in her church.

Obviously, not all its readers are named "Mary" and live in Iowa. But by knowing the *typical* reader, the editors can select articles that will truly relate to the publication's readership. While I was editorial director of teen curriculum at Wesleyan Publishing House, we surveyed summer youth camps to discover our typical reader.

Jennifer is fifteen years old, a Christian, and attends church and youth meetings faithfully. She doesn't have a regular time alone with God and rarely reads her Bible. Jennifer has a pretty good understanding of salvation, but is unsure about the denomination's emphasis on "entire sanctification." A good friend has tried sex and drugs, but she hasn't. She has a crush on a guy at church, but he acts like she doesn't exist. She has no convictions against dating a non-Christian, but is not sure where she stands about marrying a non-Christian.

So, as I dug through the pile of unsolicited manuscripts on my desk, I was only interested in articles that would effectively communicate with Jennifer.

MEETING NEEDS

All magazines have "writers guidelines" that provide detailed information on their readers. Let's look at some principles that can help us understand our readers and listeners in general. Then we'll look at some general characteristics of non-Christians. (Hopefully, many of you have a passion for effectively communicating with those outside the church.)

Felt Needs

One of the best ways to connect with our defined audience is to address their *felt* needs. My book about death for teens received a *Campus Life* "Book of the Year" award, I believe, not because it was great writing, but because it was based on the actual questions of twenty-five hundred junior and senior high students. It addressed their felt needs. And appealing to felt needs is one of the secrets of changing lives.

Psychiatrist Sigmund Freud believed that (1) organisms act only to reduce their drives; therefore all activities are categorized as direct or indirect attempts at drive reduction; and (2) activities that result in a reduction of drives are reinforced and thus repeated.

Freud seemed to put humans on an animal level, driven by drives. But to be honest, your audience *is* selfish. It responds to a message that promises to meet those basic, felt needs.

In *The Hidden Persuaders,* Vance Packard claimed that advertisers are successful when they appeal to these selfish needs and drives. He wrote that Madison Avenue is not selling products but need fulfillment.

Abraham Maslow is probably best known for his studies of these felt needs, which he arranged as a "hierarchy of needs." In his 1943 paper, "A Theory of Human Motivation," he envisioned a pyramid with the most basic needs on the bottom. One cannot progress up the levels of the pyramid until the supporting needs are satisfied. He described the first four needs as "deficit," or physiological, needs; something is missing that needs to be satisfied.

Physiological Needs

Every carbon-based life form needs oxygen, food, water, and shelter. (Notice the high percentage of fast food commercials on television!) Until these most basic needs are satisfied, one can't move up the pyramid.

Safety and Security Needs

Today, in North America, safety and security needs would include a safe neighborhood, a family in which one feels physically and socially safe, a secure job, health insurance, and a retirement fund. And so advertising and public service agencies warn us "Friends Don't Let Friends Drive Drunk," "Buckle Up," use sun screen, and so forth.

In the past, preachers have been guilty of extorting this need. I remember trembling in the pew as a fire-breathing evangelist prowled the platform telling stories of rebellious teens who walked out of church right in the middle of "Just As I Am" and were ushered into eternity by a Mac truck. Later, a popular series of films about the "last days" scared the "hell" out of teens and adults alike.

The problem is that motivation by fear generally lasts only as long as the fear.

Belonging Needs

Belonging needs include having friends, a spouse, a social group such as neighborhood association, church membership, or a bowling league. A bank in town tapped into this need by proclaiming, "You

Have a Friend at First National." I was always tempted to call and ask my "friend" to pick me up at the airport.

Christianity, however, offers to fulfill that need to belong: We become a part of God's family, we're called "children of God," we're a part of the "body of Christ," we're called His "friends."

Esteem Needs

Maslow noted our needs for respect, status, recognition, attention, reputation, appreciation, dignity, self-respect, confidence, competence, achievement, mastery, independence, and freedom. Promise to meet those needs, and you will have a ready audience.

Unfortunately, some of our hymns tear away at our esteem. "Amazing Grace" refers to us as a "wretch," and "At the Cross" describes us as a "worm" (both true, but not attractive or persuasive). It seems far better to promise that we can become "new creations" who are infinitely loved by our Creator. (Yes, stress sin, but at the very same time offer the solution of salvation.)

Maslow went on to describe "being" needs, which he called self-actualization.

"Being" Needs (Self-Actualization)

Self-actualized people tend to focus on problems outside of themselves as well as valuing such things as truth, understanding, knowledge, love, happiness, creativity, beauty, harmony, and justice.

In *Toward a Psychology of Being* (1968), Maslow redefined self-actualization as being "more integrated and less split, more open for experience, more idiosyncratic, more perfectly expressive or spontaneous, or fully functioning, more creative, more humorous, more ego-transcending, more independent of his lower needs, etc. He becomes in these episodes more truly himself, more perfectly actualizing his potentialities, closer to the core of his being, more fully human." (Maslow didn't limit "creativity" to the arts, once quipping that he preferred first-rate soup to second-rate art.)

But meeting felt needs is not enough. Each person has even deeper needs.

Faith Needs

Augustine of Hippo spoke of a restlessness that is only met in God. Another has graphically described our need for our Creator as a "God-shaped vacuum." Even if our physical, mental, social, and sexual needs are fully met, we are still haunted by that "restlessness" without God.

Indiana Wesleyan University's mission statement includes developing students who are "world changers," bringing about exactly what Maslow described: truth, understanding, knowledge, love, happiness, creativity, beauty, harmony, and justice. What an exciting, and felt-need fulfilling, message we have as "ambassadors" for Christ!

So, effective communicators begin with selfish felt needs and then skillfully make the transition into the deeper, core needs of faith.

FACING TWO NEW CHALLENGES

Two new—and encouraging—challenges face the writer and speaker in this twenty-first century: the 7.0 seismic shift from modern to postmodern thinking and "Christian" to "spiritual" cultural standards.

Bill Crouse, in *Deconstructionism: The Postmodern Cult of Hermes*, made the following distinctions between modern thought and postmodern thinking (even though postmoderns would argue it is not possible to make such arbitrary distinctions because everything is relative).

Modernism is another word for enlightenment humanism. It was a period that affirmed the existence and possibility of knowing truth by human reason alone. . . . Postmodernism in many ways is a reaction against modernism that has been brewing since the late nineteenth century. In postmodernism the intellect is replaced by will, reason by emotion, and morality by relativism. . . . In a nutshell, postmodernism says there are no universal truths valid for all people. Instead, individuals are locked into the limited perspective of their own race, gender, or ethnic group.

Despite the wailing and gnashing of teeth by those opposed to postmodern thinking, I believe there are encouraging aspects, such as the openness to faith based rather than simply fact based thinking, the rejection of modern science as god, and the realization that life is not getting better and better (as opposed to some of the aging hippies who still believe "Everything is Beautiful").

Dr. Jerry Pattengale made this point in his *Brief Guide to Objective Inquiry*, which provides this helpful chart (even though, again, postmoderns would argue it is not possible to objectively quantify such a list):

The Threats of Postmodernity to Christianity	The Opportunities of Postmodernity for Christianity
The rejection of absolute truth.	Overconfidence in human reason and technology that is broken.
Truth becomes private interpretation. There is only truth for the individual.	Closed-system naturalism is called into question.
Spirituality is unrelated to Scripture and doctrine.	Spirituality is now an acceptable pursuit.
Moral standards are obsolete.	Moral relativism makes supernaturalism more desirable.
Intensity of experience replaces depth of meaning.	Common experiences provide an avenue for discussion of common meanings.

I also see encouraging shifts from a cultural "Christianity" to a desire for a personal spirituality. For instance, Lee Strobel, a former teaching pastor at Willow Creek Community Church who specifically targets the unchurched, provided important insight with his book *Inside the Mind of Unchurched Harry and Mary.* The first six of his sixteen traits apply to those who wish to reach this group through writing and speaking.

Harry Has Rejected the Church, but that Doesn't Necessarily Mean He Has Rejected God. A quick look at the *TV Guide* or *New York Times* best-seller list proves that God is a hot topic. In the past few years, TV has brought us *Touched by an Angel*, *Seventh Heaven*, and *Joan of Arcadia*. Plus books with Christian themes have topped the *New York Times* best-sellers lists: *The Prayer of Jabez*, the fourteen-volume (and counting) *Left Behind* series, and *The Purpose-Driven Life*.

Harry Is Morally Adrift, but He Secretly Wants an Anchor. Despite all the talk of moral relativism and tolerance, one of the felt needs is security—not only physically and mentally, but spiritually and morally.

Harry Resists Rules, but Responds to Reasons. What did the prophet Isaiah declare? "Come now, and let us reason together" (Isa. 1:18, emphasis added). And what did Paul do on Mars Hills? He "reasoned" with them. This is why Peter taught, "Always be prepared to give an answer to everyone who asks you to give the reason for the hope that you have" (1 Peter 3:15).

Harry Doesn't Understand Christianity, but He's also Ignorant about what He Claims to Believe In. We live in a biblically-illiterate culture where unchurched people believe that "God helps those who help themselves" and "all men are created equal" are found in Scripture.

Former *Saturday Night Live* star Julia Sweeney in her book, *My Beautiful Loss of Faith Story*, wrote why she became an atheist at age thirty-eight. In an interview she said, "You know, like Jesus was angry a lot. When he turned all those people into pigs and made them run off a mountain, it was so hateful, not just to people but to pigs. I felt upset for the pigs!" Apparently she's as confused about God as her SNL character "Pat" was confused about his/her gender! (Check out the real story in Mark 5.)

Unfortunately abortion center bombers, those who picket military funerals with "God hates America" signs, and millionaire TV evangelists who pressure viewers to give of their limited means to build their million-dollar homes, fuel the unchurched's stereotypes of "Christians."

Harry Has Legitimate Questions About Spiritual Matters, but He Doesn't Expect Answers from Christians. Apologists such as Charles Colson, Josh McDowell, and Ravi Zacharias are proving to the world that we don't have to check our brains at the door to believe the claims of Scripture.

This is an important reason why Christian writers should seriously consider writing for the general market rather than always preaching to the choir.

Harry Doesn't just Ask, "Is Christianity True?" Often He Asks, "Does Christianity Work?" As we'll note in chapter 7, "Christian" behavior that differs little from "non-Christian" severely undercuts credibility!

With the twin challenges of postmodern thought and spiritual cultural standards, today's writers and teachers will be viewed with suspicion if they make dogmatic, absolute statements. I've found it more effective to raise questions rather than spout "answers," which, in postmodern thinking, is impossible, since there are no absolute truths—absolutely. Making this shift is difficult for me, since I grew up with the didactic methodology of "shut up and listen." So, here's an attempt from my secular newspaper column by someone who believes in absolute, propositional, biblical truth, to communicate with someone who doesn't:

ARE YOU ABSOLUTELY SURE THERE ARE NO ABSOLUTES?

Every so often an angry reader fires off a "flaming" email accusing me of being a "right-wing, conservative, hate-filled, intolerant idiot." So, I'd like to address some of those issues.

First, "idiot" is an obsolete term referring to someone with a mental capacity of a two-year-old. I'm more of a "moron," which long ago referred to someone with the mental capacity of 8–12 years old.

Second, I'm afraid—being the moron that I am—I don't understand the following tenants of the truly tolerant.

"There is no such thing as absolute truth."

Help me understand this. You're saying it's absolutely true that there's no absolute truth. And if that's true, how can you be sure your statement is truth?

"I only believe what I can perceive with my five senses."

Hmmm? Can you prove that statement by sight, smell, hearing, touch, or taste? I don't think so.

"What is right and wrong is for the individual to decide."

OK, so rapper R. Kelly, who allegedly had child pornography on his computer, shouldn't be harassed by intolerant authorities because pictures of naked twelve-year-olds are "right" for him? And that wacky Iraqi, Saddam Hussein, was simply expressing his individuality by using chemical weapons on his own people and taking his sons out for a night of torturing political prisoners.

Aren't there some things that are always wrong for everyone? And if you say "yes," aren't you admitting to a "moral absolute"? If you say "no," I'm assuming it's OK with you if I steal your wallet.

"Well, right and wrong is what a society decides it is."

Hmmm? So slavery was right for thousands of years until society recently decided it wasn't? How about segregation? Was that just fine until a majority in Congress decided it wasn't in 1964? And why are we hassling societies of China, North Korea, and Sudan for the torture and murder of religious minorities?

"No, something is wrong if it hurts other people."

Wait a minute. I thought you said there were no moral absolutes? Is that always true for all cultures? Aren't suicide bombers in the Middle East idolized as moral heroes by a part of society?

And how about the person in a mask who comes up to you, knocks you unconscious, slashes open your chest, and takes all your money? Of course I'm talking about a cardiologist. So, isn't some pain good for us? Isn't "hurt" an absolute concept? And what about sado-masochism?

"Well, you shouldn't try to change other people's beliefs."

But what if I disagree with that statement? Aren't you trying to change my beliefs? Let me get this straight. It's "right" for you to try to convince me of your ideas about "no absolute truth" and "individual morality," but it's "wrong" for me to try to take my beliefs out into the arena of public debate?

"You're just intolerant!"

So, you're saying I'm "intolerant" for voicing my beliefs, but you're "tolerant" for rejecting my views as "intolerant"?

Hmmm? Are you absolutely sure about that?

KEEPING CURRENT

Knowing the characteristics of your target audience is important, but keeping current is also vital.

National Polls

If people are doing it, you can be sure someone has conducted a poll concerning it. The U.S. Census Bureau's *Statistical Abstract of the United States*, national polls such as Gallup, news groups, and others are gold mines for discovering felt needs.

Issues and Events

Trends, social movements, issues, and fads usually appear in this order: the Internet, courts, conferences, colleges, radio, television, newspapers, advertising, music, TV sitcoms and dramas, movies, and finally, books.

If you can be one of the first to address or report on the trend, you'll have hundreds of platforms from which to share your thoughts.

Other Media

There are hundreds of other rich sources for sensing your audience's felt needs, such as personal ads, advice columns, yellow pages, entertainment pages, and even junk mail (some marketer has spent good research money to produce this junk).

Personal Contact

Look through the Christian best-seller lists and you will find one category of writers in a far greater proportion than any other—pastors. Rather than writing from a mountaintop, seaside studio, or denominational headquarters, pastors have regular contact with real people with real needs and real struggles. Keep close to people!

Benefits More Than Features

The writer or speaker who can promise to fulfill a felt need will find a ready audience. (Remember, your audience is selfish!) The same goes for churches. Most church advertising fails because it sells features rather than benefits: who's in concert Saturday night, what special event is planned for Sunday morning. Rarely do they stress the *benefits* of getting the family bathed, dressed, and into the car early on a Sunday morning. It's much easier to watch a service on TV.

But several years ago, the Episcopal Church ran a series display ads with the elements of the Eucharist, or Communion, sitting on top of a TV. The copy read, "Sony doesn't serve communion." That's a benefit!

Feelings More than Facts

As a writer, it pains me to write that subhead, but unfortunately it is true. For instance, I just saw a cola commercial. The music builds.

The camera focuses on the look of anticipation on the faces in the crowd. Suddenly flash powder explodes, lasers cut through the haze. The rock star emerges from the haze belting out the soft drink jingle. The audience screams. A quick close-up of a vendor carrying a tray of the product—and that's the end of a multi-million-dollar commercial.

Nothing about the cost, calories, or even results of a national taste test—only the implied message that the rock star and his fans love the cola. So, the ad agency is betting millions that the average teen desperately wants to feel popular, accepted, and part of the "in" crowd. Feelings, not facts, sell products.

Or as a grad professor used to quip, "Psycho logic beats plain logic any day of the week."

If we are going to effectively present the gospel, we must know our audience and the needs that drive them. And next, we need to present this in an orderly fashion.

Not only was the Teacher wise, but also
he imparted knowledge to the people.
He pondered and searched out and
set in order many proverbs.

Ecclesiastes 12:9

3
KNOWING THE
TECHNIQUES
OF GOOD
ORGANIZATION

Both Luke and Paul were inspired by the Holy Spirit to put God's truth in written form. And yet there are some very real differences in their approaches.

> Many have undertaken to draw up an account of the things that have been fulfilled among us, just as they were handed down to us by those who from the first were eyewitnesses and servants of the word. Therefore, since I myself have carefully investigated everything from the beginning, it seemed good also to me to write an orderly account for you, most excellent Theophilus, so that you may know the certainty of the things you have been taught. (Luke 1:1–4)

> [Paul] writes the same way in all his letters. . . . His letters contain some things that are hard to understand. (2 Peter 3:16)

Again, both are equally inspired, but one is much easier to read than the other.

Paul probably paced back and forth as he dictated his insights to a scribe. In the apostle's excitement, the words poured out as his poor scribe tried to keep up with pen and parchment. His sentences tend to be lengthy and complex, and some do require real effort to understand.

Luke, however, deliberately researched his subject and organized the material. And, I even think, he wrote several drafts to make sure God's message is in the best literary form as possible. (Greek scholars consider Luke's work the most beautiful writing in the New Testament.)

Both writings are "God-breathed and . . . useful for teaching, rebuking, correcting and training in righteousness" (2 Tim. 3:16). But one style is much easier to read—and understand—than the other. And if it's easy to read, you can be sure it was hard to write!

WRITE AND REWRITE YOUR MESSAGE

Unfortunately, in our society, if it's not written clearly on a sixth-grade level, God's message will not get a reading or hearing. So, let me suggest that you write fast and rewrite slow. Write the first draft, typing just as fast as you can keep up with your thoughts. Don't worry about spelling, grammar, or syntax. If you come to a point where you can't think of just the right word, tap a series of Xs and keep on typing. Every time you stop to check your dictionary or thesaurus, you break the flow of inspiration.

Then, and this is the secret to writing, rewrite. Write the first draft with your heart, but rewrite subsequent drafts with your head.

And be sure to give yourself a few days between writing and rewriting. For instance, when my daughter was born, she wasn't the red, scrawny, prune-faced little creature like all other newborns. Faith was perfect. But several days later after I got the photos back, I realized, "She *is* a red, scrawny, prune-faced little creature like all the other newborns." In the same way, after we have labored to produce the greatest writing since the book of Revelation, we tend to overlook the congenital defects in our first draft. Come back a few days later to begin the process of putting your manuscript into a publishable form.

LIMIT YOUR MESSAGE

As a junior-higher, I dreaded my pastor's prayers at carry-in dinners. By the time he was done praying for every shut-in in the congregation, the entire admissions list at Community Hospital, every missionary in the United Methodist Church, and the heads of state of each member of the United Nations, the fifteen tuna casseroles and six pots of baked beans were cold.

And every Sunday, his sermons covered more ground than his prayers: from Genesis to maps! His messages failed, not because of poor ideas, but because of too many good ideas on too broad a subject. The same is true with writers. I often joke at writers conferences that I've seen many wonderful articles, but unfortunately, they are all in the same manuscript.

The topic must be restricted so the focus is sharp and clear. (Don't you hate it when the video projector is just a bit out of focus!) Luke researched "everything from the beginning," but he certainly didn't write everything from the beginning. John closed his gospel noting that "Jesus did many other things as well. If every one of them were written down, I suppose that even the whole world would not have room for the books that would be written" (John 21:25).

For instance, "God" is too broad a topic and would need a manuscript the length of the *Encyclopaedia Britannica* to cover it adequately. And you'd need a year-long sermon series to cover the subject.

"God's love" is better but still requires a book the size of *Oxford's Unabridged Dictionary* or a thirteen-week Sunday school class if covered well.

"God's love expressed in tragedy" is getting there. The topic is continuing to become more narrow, focused, and specific.

"Sharing God's love with the terminally ill" has a good chance for success. We can see specific individuals, and we know how helpless we feel in not knowing what to say to those dying of cancer. The narrower the focus, the better! (There is, of course, a limit. "Sharing God's love with whooping cough patients in Toledo" is probably too limited.)

William Zinsser in *On Writing Well* suggested we look at our article or speech as a pie. As much as I love pecan pie, I probably can't—or shouldn't—eat the whole pie. Zinsser wrote, "Decide what corner of your subject you are going to bite off, and be content to cover it well and stop. You can always come back another day and bite off another corner."

The challenge, then, is to provide our readers and listeners with a serving that is satisfying, but doesn't cause feelings of gas and bloating.

An excellent discipline, then, is to distill the topic down to just three words. For instance in our example, "compassion communicates love." For this book, my three words are Aristotle's three elements of effective communication: logos (intelligence), pathos (intensity), and ethos (integrity). Everything from the introduction to the final chapter must directly relate to those three words. And anything that doesn't, no matter how clever or creative, must be scrapped. (I deleted more than fifty pages, but Philip Yancey in the first draft of *In His Image* deleted 150 pages!)

ORGANIZE YOUR MESSAGE

I lived in a girl's dorm for six years (my wife was resident director). The dorm and a house I was using for an office were just a block apart. But in the name of progress, the university tore up the road between them and planted a lovely garden with plants and flowering trees I can't pronounce. It looked absolutely beautiful, but was absolutely frustrating. On rainy days or days I needed to haul something back and forth, I now had to drive three blocks when I used to have to drive only one block.

Flowery writing and speaking without organization are equally frustrating. Try to visualize your message as the express lane of a freeway—no exits, no entry ramps—a straight path to your destination.

Here are some outlines that create such an expressway à la I-94 through Chicago.

Case History

I. Description of the problem

II. Anecdote of problem's solution

III. Precisely how it was solved

IV. Proof of solution

V. Challenge (You can do it, too!)

Hard News

Journalistic reporting—and news releases for your church—relies on the "inverted pyramid." The lead or first paragraph must include who, what, where, when, why, and how of the event. (This first paragraph is sometimes called a "lede," which was used years ago to distinguish it from molten lead used at the time to make printing plates.) Each subsequent paragraph includes less and less important information.

It's designed in this fashion so if the editor has room for only one paragraph, everything essential to the story is included in the first paragraph. He or she can also cut it at any other paragraph and still have a well-organized article, no matter how long.

And, it works well for sermons! If the listener nods off after just five minutes, he or she has at least gotten the gist of the message.

Personality Story

I. Lead anecdote illustrating person's personality

II. Present status (who, what, where person is)

III. Big "flashback" (goes back and explains how person arrived in his or her present state)

IV. Closing anecdote (refers back to lead anecdote)

Notice that it's not written in chronological order ("John Doe was born in 1952 and . . .") but dives right into the core of his personality. Here's a very short example I wrote for a teen magazine several years ago:

[Lead anecdote] Amy Fletcher is like most fourteen-year-old girls. She fights with her two brothers, loves clothes, and wants a car for her sixteenth birthday. And Marysville Junior High is "ycchh."

[Present status] But she's also very different. She loves broccoli, cauliflower, and liver. Plus, she has sung with Sandi Patty, the Imperials, Doug Oldham, Danny Gaither, Dino, and just about everyone in Christian music at the Dove Awards.

But Amy has managed to remain "just another kid" at her church in Michigan. She's active in the youth group and looks forward to being with her Christian friends at church parties. Her favorite singers are Sandi Patty and Steve Green. And she enjoys playing the flute, sax, and piano.

She does seem like just another kid until she opens her mouth. Suddenly she's an up-and-coming singer with three albums and as many octaves to her credit.

"My voice just keeps getting higher and lower as I get older." She handles Sandi Patty's "We Shall Behold Him" and Twila Paris's "The Warrior is a Child" with equal ease.

[Big flashback] Amy's career began when, as a child of seven, she was the letter "C" in her church's Christmas program. The music director at her church sensed she had a real talent, helped her record a demo, and began making calls to friends in the music industry. Before she knew it, Amy was singing at the Crystal Cathedral, on Christian television networks, and with major artists at Christian music festivals.

What would she like to be doing in ten years? "Let's see. I'll be twenty-four. I guess I'd like to have won a Grammy, a Dove, and still be singing. I want to get closer to my audiences and have them get closer to God. The best thing is seeing kids getting saved as a result of a concert. I guess I just want to keep doing what I'm doing."

[Closing anecdote] With that Amy is begging her mom to let her change out of her concert dress and into some jeans. Yes, Amy is still like most fourteen-year-old girls.

Persuasive Article

If you ever took a high school debate class or college class on rhetoric, you probably learned this classical form of persuasion.

I. State problem
II. Review facts
III. Review possible solutions
IV. Recommend one solution
V. Support reasons
VI. Spell out likely effects

However, in today's culture that is driven on how our minds work and process information, a new outline for persuasive messages has emerged.

I. Recommend solution
II. State problem

III. Support reasons

IV. Review facts

V. Review possible solutions

VI. Spell out like effects

Say, for instance, you're a pastor of an older church without air-conditioning. (Yes, there are still some holdouts who believe if the Upper Room didn't have air-conditioning, neither should their church!) Here's how your appeal letter would read if you were using pure logic:

> [State problem] As you know, the temperature in the sanctuary has reached ninety-five degrees the past six Sundays. [Review facts] The elderly and families with children are staying away because of the unbearable heat. [Review possible solutions] We could move the services outside in the shade, hand out fans, or air-condition the sanctuary. Rain and distractions from traffic and passersby would make outdoor services unworkable, and the janitor refuses to move the grand piano out onto the sidewalk. [Recommend one solution] Air-conditioning would be the ideal solution. [Supporting reasons] The elderly could enjoy the padded pews, the children could play once more in the nursery, and the grand piano would not have to be moved out onto the sidewalk. [Spell out likely effects] Yes, air-conditioning would bring back hundreds of parishioners who can't take the heat.

However, the order would be completely changed if you were using popular logic.

> [Recommend one solution] Air-conditioning is needed in our church. [State problem] As you know, the temperature in the sanctuary has reached ninety-five degrees the past six

Sundays. [Supporting reasons] The elderly and children could once again be a part of our services. [Review facts] As it is, the elderly and families with children are staying away because of the unbearable heat. [Review possible solutions] We could move the services outside in the shade, hand out fans, or air-condition the sanctuary. Rain and distractions from traffic and passersby would make outdoor services unworkable, and the janitor refuses to move the grand piano out onto the sidewalk. [Spell out likely effects] Yes, air-conditioning would bring back hundreds of parishioners who can't take the heat.

Self-help

Walk into any bookstore and look around. You'll be overwhelmed by the number of self-help books: *Twelve Secrets to This*, *Seven Ways to Do That*, *The Purpose-Driven Other Thing*. They do appeal to the felt needs we discussed in the previous chapter (and let's say it again: your audience is selfish). And self-help articles or talks are incredibly easy to write.

I. Anecdote of person(s) in need of help
II. Steps to solution with anecdotes at each point
III. Anecdote/testimony of an overcomer

That's it! Now go write a best seller. Create a dynamic speaking ministry.

Trend Piece

If you're writing or speaking about a political or moral change in society, you may want to use this outline:

I. Lead (anecdote, shocking facts, etc.)
II. Description of present status

III. Explanation of cause(s)

IV. Evaluation

V. Forecast, possible consequences

ADVERTISE YOUR MESSAGE

No matter what genre or format you use, the very first words must sell your book or speech. Most editors I know read only one or two paragraphs. If the piece hasn't grabbed them by the throat or heart, neither will it their readers, so they reach for a rejection slip. And if the first words of your message don't captivate your listeners, like Elvis, their minds will have left the building.

And, as a writer, you're not competing with only other articles or books. You're competing with the Internet, electronic Solitaire, five hundred channels of cable TV, the newspaper, and watching the new neighbors move in.

In speaking, you must overcome the temptation of your listeners to daydream about work at the office they need to do the next day, if they set the timer correctly on the oven or DVD recorder, why doesn't the woman sitting in front of them do something different with her 1950s hairdo, et cetera, et cetera.

You must convince your potential audience that your message is more important than these distractions. And you have to do this within the first few sentences.

CRAFT A COMPELLING LEAD

A Good Lead Attracts Attention

The lead must create a sense of anticipation that one of those felt needs described in chapter 2 is going to be fulfilled with your message or lesson. If it doesn't, your audience will tune out.

Think of a lead as one of those screaming announcers on car commercials: "AT CRAZY CARL'S CAR CORRAL, WE'LL PUT YOU

IN A BRAND NEW CAR WITH NO MONEY DOWN, NO PAY-
MENTS FOR THREE MONTHS. PLUS . . ."

Dr. Dennis Hensley listed his top ten attention grabbers:

Competition
Conflict
Controversy
Consequences
Familiar or famous people
Human interest
Humor
A common problem
Success
The unknown, weird, bizarre

Madison Avenue has its own list of never-miss human interest:

Love
Sex
Hate
Fear
Vanity
Selfishness
Ambition
Immorality
Evildoing
Cruelty

Here are some ways to put those interests to work:

An Anecdote: Make it humorous, dramatic, or suspenseful.
A Shocking Statement or Quote: Just be sure you verify it.
A Question that Addresses a Felt Need: "Do you ever feel alone

in a church of two thousand?" "When was the last time you and your spouse had some time away?" "Do you want to change lives in person and print?"

A Memory-inducing Anecdote: Just be sure you know your audience and that it's a memory that they can recall. "Do you remember where you were when John F. Kennedy was assassinated?" will only work for aging baby boomers.

Jumping Right into the Middle of the Action: A friend asked me to help him write his personal experience with the exact kind of injury that made Joni Eareckson Tada a quadriplegic. However, he walked out of the hospital less than a month later, since a world-famous neurosurgeon "just happened" to be visiting a friend in a tiny hospital in Cadillac, Michigan. It's an amazing story, but Mike began his article, "I was born in Cadillac, Michigan, and attended Cadillac High School, where I was on the track team, and . . ." I suggested he jump right into the middle of the story as outlined in the section of personal experience stories:

I opened my eyes and looked around as I floated face-down in the eerie silence of Cadillac Lake. I couldn't feel any pain as I mentally checked myself out.

Just seconds ago I had dived into the lake, hoping to swim underwater and give my mom and sister, who were sunbathing on a raft, a good scare.

Now I was the one scared.

I must have bumped my head on something. I just need to wait a second to get my bearings.

After a moment I put every ounce of strength and mental energy into lifting my head out of the water. Nothing happened. I strained to turn my head so I could gasp for air, but the surface of the water seemed just a quarter of an inch away from my mouth.

I tried to fight panic as I remembered my lifeguard training. I knew if I passed out, I wouldn't be able to hold my breath any longer. My lungs would fill with water, and I'd be gone.

Come on, Mom! Notice me! I'm running out of air!

Gradually the lake bottom began turning gray. My lungs felt as if they were being crushed. I closed my eyes and realized, *They're not going to reach me in time.*

OK, it's a first-person story, so obviously we know he survives to write it, but hopefully the reader is now more fully engaged in the story.

Conversation: An article on the intrinsic differences between males and females was starting to read like a term paper, so I transferred the information into a Sunday school class discussion. The article began with the student trying to stump the teacher with a difficult question. Various students added their opinions and questions. Suddenly, the potentially academic article became a lively interchange of information.

Summary: Tell your audience what you're going to tell them, without letting the whole cat out of the bag.

A Good Lead Establishes the Subject

Within a few seconds, your audience should know the exactly what you're writing about.

A Good Lead Sets the Tone

Is this a humorous piece? Is it a scholarly work? Is it a touching personal experience story? Is it a thriller? Again, your audience should know sooner rather than later.

A Good Lead Doesn't Make Promises It Can't Keep

Back to our car commercial. You know very well there's some kind of catch or a disclaimer at the end of the commercial read at five hundred words per minute:

"Somerestrictionsapplybasedoncreditratingandinventoryavail-
ability. Doesnotincludedealerprepanddestinationcharges.
Notvalidonsunnydaysoreven-numbereddates. . . ."

If you don't fulfill the promises made in the lead or introduction,
your audience will feel just as deceived. You can certainly build anticipation by withholding key points or ideas until later in the message,
but make sure you *deliver* later.

CREATIVELY TITLE YOUR MESSAGE

Writing a great title for a book or sermon is often a challenge. Here's
how I brainstorm titles. I start with the subject in a circle in the middle of
a blank page, then start adding circles for synonyms, homonyms,
rhyming words, associated nouns and verbs, biblical phrases, familiar
quotations, or song and movie titles. It looks like nuclear fission—circles
branching out from other circles. I brainstorm until fission slows down,
and then I start looking for relationships between the various circles.

For instance, I was asked to write an article for a funeral director on
the importance of showing emotion. I wrote *grief* in the middle circle and
fission-ed out to topics such as *emotions, feelings, funeral home, ceme-
tery, burial plot,* and so forth. I then made the connection between
feelings and *burial* and came up with "Don't Bury Your Feelings."

Here are some of my favorite titles that came out of this atomic
reaction:

Synonyms
On diversity: "One Nation Under the Supreme
Being of Your Choice"
Antonyms
On faith healing: "Healing: Faith or Fake?"

Homonyms

On porn vs. passion: "Reel or Real Sex?"

On cult abuse: "Sects and Violence"

On irritations in staff ministry: "Staff or Staph?"

Rhyming Words

On some Christians' unhealthy emphasis on demon activity: "Demons: Possession or Obsession?"

On the mental health benefits of touch: "Mood Altering Hugs."

Associated Nouns and Verbs

On the pros and cons of the book: "*Harry Potter:* The Good, the Bad, the Muggly" ("Muggles" are humans without magical powers in the book.)

On the breakdown of the family: "The Nuclear Family Bomb"

On the euthanasia message of an Oscar-winning film: "*Million Dollar Baby* Throws in the Towel"

Familiar Phrases, Titles

On spiritual warfare: "Other World Wrestling Federation"

On the importance of encouragement: "Affirmative Action"

On humorous inspiration: "Fruitcake for the Soul"

On setting goals as a writer: "The Purpose-Driven Writer"

On babysitting our granddaughter: "The Papoose-Driven Life"

On kidney stones: "All Things Must Pass" (Sorry!)

Movie Titles

On the battle over genetic engineering: "The Clone Wars"

On the true meaning of Christmas: "How Christmas Saved a Grinch"

Most of all, have fun and let the nuclear reaction begin.

Admittedly, organizing an article or lesson is not the most exciting part of the process, but it is one of the most important. The effectiveness of persuasion depends on "an orderly account."

4

KNOWING THE TECHNIQUES OF GOOD WRITING AND SPEAKING

Best-selling author and popular newspaper columnist Richard Lederer has made a career of poking fun at bad writing from student papers to political speeches.

> The Gorgons had long snakes in their hair. They looked like women only more horrible.

> In midevil [sic] times . . . people put on morality plays about ghosts, goblins, virgins, and other mythical creatures.

> The Magna Carta provided that no free man should be hanged twice for the same offense.

Is it any wonder that the prophet Habakkuk wrote, "Write down the revelation and make it plain" (2:2)?

I spotted these errors while editing manuscripts at Wesleyan Publishing House:

"Then weeping, her hands clasped in prayer." Her hands were weeping?! It should have read, "Then weeping, she clasped her hands

in prayer."

"Having just preached a powerful sermon, the seekers at the altar were a joyous sight." So, the seekers preached their own invitation?! Make that "After the pastor preached a powerful sermon, the seekers at the altar were a joyous sight." Make sure you have noun-verb agreement.

But here's one of the worst examples:

It is our earnest prayer that against the backdrop of our troubled times, the Fifth General Conference of The Wesleyan Church, with the warm inspiration of nightly rallies, the fresh uplift of renewed friendships, the rewarding richness of Christian fellowship, the sober intensity of serious business sessions and the open-hearted renewing of the Church's commitment to a redemptive ministry will be a life-changing experience for each delegate and for the many other ministers and laypeople, members and friends who gather there.

That's one eighty-one-word sentence, which brings me to the first point in a checklist for readability.

1. Check the Reading Level of Your Message

Most Americans read on a sixth-grade level, so it's important to keep the level of writing as close to sixth grade as possible. In the NIV, the teachings of Jesus are at a seventh-grade level. (It's difficult to accurately delineate Christ's grade level since He spoke in Aramaic, was recorded in Greek, and then translated into English.) In contrast, an Internal Revenue Service publication had a reading level of thirty-ninth grade! No wonder we can't understand those forms!

In Microsoft Word, you can check "Readability Statistics" by going to Tools, then Spelling and Grammar. Click on Options and check Readability Statistics. After you have completed the spell check, a box will appear that gives you the Flesch-Kincaid Grade

Level and Flesch Reading Ease scores.

You can also compute the reading level manually using the Gunning Fog Index. For instance, for that eighty-one-word sentence,

(1) Determine the average number of words per sentence. (81 words)

(2) Count the number of three-syllable words in the first one hundred words. Don't count proper names, combinations of simple words (e.g., open-hearted), or words made three syllables by "ed," "es," or "ing." (14 three-syllable words)

(3) Add 1 and 2, then multiply by 4.

According to Microsoft Word, that sentence has a reading level of thirty-sixth grade. That's twenty years of graduate work! When figured manually, we get a reading level of thirty-eighth grade. (I should hold myself to the same standards, so this book is written at an eighth-grade level with the average sentence length fourteen words. That's two grades higher than the average reader, but you're not "average," right?)

Paul warned against foggy writing almost two thousand years ago.

If you speak to people in words they don't understand, how will they know what you are saying? You might as well be talking into empty space. . . . I would rather speak five understandable words to help others than ten thousand words in an unknown language. (1 Cor. 14:9, 19 NLT)

Best-selling author Charlie Shedd claimed the rule of simplicity "must be applied severely by (a) ministers, (b) those with conservative backgrounds, and (c) eggheads hung up on their on intellectualism."

Francis Schaeffer, arguably one of the most intellectual writers of the twentieth century, wrote, "The most profound things are the most simple. And the most simple are the most profound."

And Arthur Kudner put it this way:

Big long words name little things.

All big things have little names.
Learn to use little words in a big way.
Big words often fool little people.

So, if the Son of God can communicate eternal truth at a seventh-grade level, who are we to write or speak at any higher level?

2. Delete Everything that Doesn't Directly and Naturally Apply to Your Three-Word Synopsis
See chapter 3.

3. Rearrange Any Paragraphs or Sections that Are Out of Logical, Natural Order
Use one of the outlines in chapter 3 to provide the order.

4. Make Sure the Logic Is Sound
We'll discuss this in the next chapter.

5. Check for Poor Word Choice

6. Use Easily Understood Words
Nancy Sommers wrote in *I Stand Here Writing*, "I was the kind of student who loved words, words out of context, words that swirled around inside my mouth, words like exacerbate, undulating, lugubrious, and zeugma. . . . I would try to write zeugmas whenever I could, exacerbating, my already lugubrious prose." Huh?!

Use easily understood words. Write to express, not to impress.

The most familiar words are ten short ones: *the, of, and, to, a, in, that, it, is, I*. They make up 25 percent of all that is written and spoken in English.

Even the prestigious Yale University has discovered through its research that the most persuasive words in the English language are short, simple words: *you, now, guarantee, results, money, easy, love, health, save, free, discovery,* and *proven.*

That's why Richard Lederer wrote,

When you speak and write, there is no law that says you have to use big words. Short words are as good as long ones, and short, old words—like *sun* and *grass* and *home*—are best of all. A lot of small words, more than you might think, can meet your needs with a strength, grace, and charm that large words do not have.

Big words can make the way dark for those who read what you write and hear what you say. Small words cast their clear light on big things—*night* and *day, love* and *hate, war* and *peace,* and *life* and *death.* Big words at times seem strange to the eye and the ear and the mind and the heart. Small words are the ones we seem to have known from the time we were born, like the hearth fire that warms the home.

Short words are bright like sparks that glow in the night, prompt like the dawn that greets the day, sharp like the blade of a knife, hot like salt tears that scald the cheek, quick like moths that flit from flame to flame, and terse like the dart and sting of a bee.

Here is a sound rule: Use small, old words where you can. They will not let you down. (Lederer, Richard. *The Miracle of Language.* New York: Pocket Books, 1991.)

Christian writers and pastors are probably the worst at not using easily understood words, especially when communicating to the unchurched. We use terms like *anointed, baptism, carnal nature, deliverance, eschatology, foreknowledge, gnostic, hermeneutic,* and the rest of the theological alphabet. Forcing ourselves to explain words like *salvation* and *sanctification,* without using church-ese, actually forces us to understand the concepts more fully. (Often we simply define jargon with more jargon.)

Having small children helped me to translate theology 101 and 201 to a five-year-old. It's also helped my own understanding of these terms we banter around. For instance, one day Faith came home from Lakeview Christian School and announced that her six-month-old brother was going to hell.

"Paul is going to hell?" I tried to calmly ask.

"Yeah, Paul's going to hell."

"Why is that?"

"Because he hasn't asked Jesus Christ into his life as his personal Savior."

I had the chance to explain the high-sounding concept of prevenient grace to my five-year-old, and by doing that, I found that I understood it better myself without defining it with other theological jargon.

Keep in mind your audience is likely reading at a six-grade level, with a vocabulary of only ten thousand words—three thousand of which they use regularly. Here's a rule I've tried to observe: If I don't hear it on TV, I don't use it. (Yes, I know about the dangers of "dumbing down" our message, but I also know, like Lederer argued, the small words are the powerful words.)

Here's my attempt to put salvation into easily understood words and concepts that communicate with those outside the church. (Notice that I've defined "atone" and "sin" in the text.)

LOOKING FOR LOVE

Many people spend their lives, as the song goes, "Lookin' for love in all the wrong places." So, how do we find real, lasting love?

Love Comes from God

"Dear friends, let us love one another, for love comes from God." (1 John 4:7)

Many people think that God is only interested in rules. But God is all about love. Jesus, God the Son, reminds us of the most important "rule":

"'Love the Lord your God with all your heart and with all your soul and with all your mind.' This is the first and greatest commandment. And the second is like it: 'Love your neighbor as yourself.'" (Matt. 22:37–39)

"OK," we say. "That sounds good." But we seem powerless to love like that.

Those who say, "I love God," and hate their brothers or sisters, are liars; for those who do not love a brother or sister whom they have seen, cannot love God whom they have not seen. The commandment we have from him is this: those who love God must love their brothers and sisters also. (1 John 4:20–21 NRSV)

The Power to Love Comes from God

Everyone who loves has been born of God and knows God. Whoever does not love does not know God, because God is love. This is how God showed his love among us: He sent his one and only Son into the world that we might live through him. This is love: not that we loved God, but that he loved us and sent his Son as an atoning sacrifice for our sins. (1 John 4:7–10)

Anything we have done that is not loving separates us from a loving God. We don't have to murder or commit armed robbery to "sin." Sin is simply breaking God's commandment to fully love Him and others.

If we claim to be without sin, we deceive ourselves and the truth is not in us. (1 John 1:8)

But His only Son, Jesus Christ, died and rose again to atone for our unloving behavior (1 John 2:1–2). Atone means to make "at-one." When we confess our lack of love (sin) and believe that Christ has died and risen for our sin, we are forgiven and are "at one" with God and His love (1 John 1:9).

God abides in those who confess that Jesus is the Son of God, and they abide in God (1 John 4:15).

The Power to Love Unselfishly Comes from God

Love from God is not earned—it is a free gift—but it is also learned.

No one has ever seen God; but if we love one another, God lives in us and his love is made complete in us. (1 John 4:12)

We get to know God and His love better through reading his love letter (the Bible), talking to Him (prayer), and being with those who also love Him (the church). And the better we know God, the easier it is for us to obey His commandment to love Him and others.

This is love for God: to obey his commands. And his commands are not burdensome, for everyone born of God overcomes the world [of hate]. (1 John 5:3–4)

If you'd like to know more about God and His great love, please feel free to e-mail me at jim@jameswatkins.com.

7. Use Specific Words

The more concrete our words, the easier it is for our readers and listeners to identify with the message. For instance, the word *dessert* doesn't really do anything for me. "Ice cream" is better, but I still can't taste it. I *can* see, smell, feel, and taste a "mint chocolate chip sundae drenched in fudge syrup."

Remember, good communication involves all five senses. For instance, Philip Yancey wrote, "Old Testament Jews understood the full impact of words like atonement and forgiveness: they watched as the priest slid the knife across the spurting artery of a fear-stricken lamb." I feel those words, rather than just hearing them.

8. Use Picture Nouns and Action Verbs

Think of adjectives and adverbs as seasoning. For instance, as a teen I decided to help make spaghetti sauce while my mom was in the hospital. I carefully added the tomato paste and tomato sauce and the one-quarter cup of garlic. Not exactly being "Mr. Food," I didn't realize the recipe called for *chopped* garlic, so I poured in a quarter cup of *powdered* garlic. My family had bad breath for two weeks! So, treat adjectives and adverbs like garlic. Use them very sparingly.

Be generous, though, with action verbs. Active verbs provide energy, vigor, and pizzazz to your writing and speaking. Avoid lazy verbs like *has, had, was, is, are, were, seem,* and *said.*

And avoid passive verbs such as "The prayer was said by the pastor." "The pastor said the prayer" is a bit better but doesn't provide power like "The pastor groaned the prayer." Now, there's emotional context; he's in emotional and spiritual agony. Change it to "The pastor droned the prayer," and the emotional context is just the opposite: mechanical, bored, apathetic.

So, rather than trying to prop up a lazy verb with an adverb, use a powerful verb. John didn't "run fast," he "sprinted."

9. Use Only Necessary Words

Replacing an adverb and a weak verb with one powerful verb makes your writing tight. And remember, we are writing for many who don't enjoy reading. To effectively communicate, we must give them more for less.

Get rid of redundant and useless words: *continue on, end result, advance planning, restore again, visible to the eye, blue in color, viable option, join together, due to the fact that, absolutely essential, and sum total.* Each word must pull its own weight.

10. Use a Variety of Words

Avoid using the same word over and over, unless for deliberate effect. Run, walk, jog, saunter, perambulate to your nearest bookstore for a good thesaurus or use one of the many online. The purpose is to find other *familiar, easily understood* words for those pet words that keep cropping up. (And, whatever you do, don't use perambulate!)

11. Use the Right Sounding Words

Effective communication uses the sounds of words to create precise emotions. If you want to create a comforting sound, the words themselves must *sound* comforting. Wilfred Funk surveyed a cross-section of teachers to find the most beautiful words in the English language. They are *chimes, dawn, golden, hush, lullaby, luminous, mellow, mist, murmuring, tranquil, cascade, glimmer, shimmer, glow, silvery, bouquet, rapture, sheen,* and *splendid.*

Use soft consonants as "Sentences float feather-soft over the page."

If, however, you want to create conflict, let hard consonants grind, crunch, and collide as "Words scrape across the page like glaciers crushing everything in their path." Use some of what Funk discovered were the worst-sounding words in the English language: *cacophony, crunch, flatulent, gripe, jazz, phlegmatic, plump, plutocrat, sap, treachery, manure, pus, guts, cancer, belch, verbose, whore, vomit,* and *scum.* (Yech!)

12. Use the Best Word

Mark Twain observed, "The difference between the right word and the almost-right word is the difference between the lightning and the lightning bug." (I would have played on the parallelism of lightning *bolt* and lightning bug, but it's still a great quote.) Don't settle for a good word when the best word is still to be discovered in the dictionary.

13. Use Inclusive Language

Before the 1960s, *man* was assumed to be a generic word for both men and women. *Mankind* included both genders. Not so today. To avoid alienating half the population, always use inclusive language. But don't use the very groovy "s/him" from the 70s or the awkward "his or her." The easiest, most natural way to be inclusive is to use plural forms. Instead of "A writer can use his or her skills to avoid sexist language," write "Writers can use their skills to avoid sexist language." And substitute *humankind* for *mankind.*

14. Check for Unclear Sentences

Avoid those bloopers from the beginning of the chapter! Do the noun and verb agree? Is there any way the sentence could be misunderstood?

15. Use Only One Idea per Sentence

That eighty-one-word sentence we discussed earlier can be made easier to read by using the powerful key between the comma and the slash—the period!

The Fifth General Conference of The Wesleyan Church will be a time of serious business sessions. But we are praying for much more. We want each delegate and visitor to be inspired by the nightly rallies and uplifted by rich fellowship. We want all to renew their desire to share the gospel in our troubled times.

Nothing is lost, and the reading level drops from thirty-sixth grade to seventh grade! (It's actually lower since *serious* and *visitor* are common three-syllable words.)

16. Use Short Sentences

The sentence above now contains fourteen words, compared to eighty-one! A fifteen-word limit is a good goal. Long, lumbering sentences "fog" up your writing.

17. Use Punch Lines in Writing and Speaking

Even the most serious writing needs a punch line. (Notice how "A punch line is needed, even in the most serous writing" loses its impact.)

18. Check for Good Paragraphs

As you learned in English class, effective paragraphs begin with a "topic sentence." What's the main point of your paragraph? This is followed by sentences that develop and support the main idea of the paragraph with facts, details, examples, etc. The paragraph ends by restating the main idea of your paragraph.

19. Use Only One Point per Paragraph

This will help you to keep the second point.

20. Use Short Paragraphs

Since most Americans don't read for pleasure, we need to make the writing *look* like less. Long paragraphs may look too intimidating, but a series of short paragraphs makes the text appear more manageable by creating more "white space."

In each paragraph, the first sentence must grab the reader's attention. The last drives home the point.

21. Use Transitions to Tie Paragraphs and Thoughts Together

Think of transitions as the shock absorbers that smooth out otherwise bumpy writing and speaking. They cushion the jolt from thought to thought, sentence to sentence, paragraph to paragraph, and section to section.

One can simply use single words to accomplish this: *meanwhile, nevertheless, therefore, consequently, furthermore, finally, naturally, however*, or *but.* These are not the best, but they're certainly better than a message that jumps and bolts from one idea to the other.

More creative approaches include using key words as a common denominator to link the paragraphs. We see this often in the psalms, particularly 118:

> Give thanks to the LORD, for he is good;
>   his love endures forever.
> Let Israel say:
>   "His love endures forever."
> Let the house of Aaron say:
>   "His love endures forever."
> Let those who fear the LORD say:
>   "His love endures forever."

Time and locale can smooth out copy: "When they finally arrived at the hotel"; "Her suitcase was still unpacked when . . ."; "Once settled in . . .".

Moods can take the reader from one idea to another. "Her smile quickly inverted into a frown"; "Slowly, the hurt began to unwrap from around her heart."

When a change in view is needed, try "Many agree with . . ."; "Critics, however, point out . . ."; "But Joe Smith has a simple reply to . . .".

Simply numbering your points cues the reader that a new idea is coming. (Thank the Lord for PowerPoint!)

Using subheads (as throughout this book) provides smooth transitions from one topic to the next.

Carrying a specific object, illustration, or motif throughout the message serves to tie the entire work together. We see this in Scripture, where blood sacrifice for sin is a scarlet thread weaving its way through virtually every book. Moses' staff is an object that ties the book of Exodus together: at the burning bush, at the confrontations with Pharaoh, at the Red Sea, at the rock that miraculously brings forth water, and eventually as a relic in the ark of the covenant. In Philippians, the word *joy* ties Paul's letter together.

I've italicized the various transitions in the following essay.

24K CROSSES

They just don't make crosses like they used to.

Two thousand years ago, the Romans handcrafted them out of real wood—rugged, solid, durable—stained with natural colors. Awe and respect were felt for the manufacturers of these creations.

But like many products, most crosses today are machine-made and mass-produced by managers who look only at the bottom line of numbers and dollars. Solid, rough wood has been replaced by polished veneer in walnut, oak, or cherry—coordinated of course, to match the padded pews.

For a more contemporary look, there are polished aluminum, Plexiglas, and fiberglass designs in decorator colors. Who can forget the plastic glow-in-the-dark crosses awarded for Sunday school promotions?

Even mail-order jewelry catalogs feature "dignified yet richly designed in 24k gold-filled or sterling silver, with matching Venetian box link chains. Perfect for baptisms, communion, or wedding gift." One offers "the tranquility of this beautiful platinum-plated cross."

Another promises "a gold electro-plated cross with a micro-dot of the entire Bible in the center so you can have the peace of God's Word near you throughout the day."

They just don't make crosses like they used to.

When Christ told his disciples to take up their crosses and follow him, he wasn't talking about 24-karat jewelry. He had in mind a rough beam, splintered and stained with sweat, blood, and drugged wine. No wonder the idea caused Peter to "rebuke" the

Lord for such a statement. That's why Paul called the cross a "stumbling block to Jews and foolishness to Gentiles."

And so the organized church began to sand off the rough, irritating edges. The old stains were stripped away. The cross needed "improved marketing" and better "packaging." Two thousand years later, the cross has been so well repositioned that it's now available in the most elegant jewelry stores and worn by the most respectable and fashionable of socialites.

But in doing so, has the cross of Christ been emptied of its power? Has this instrument of death been refashioned into a beautiful wall hanging or piece of costume jewelry? And have its followers also become only thin veneer? Have souls become lacquered with coats of high-gloss varnish so the blood, living water, and new wine rarely penetrate the exterior?

They just don't make crosses like they used to.

Christ is not asking us to take up a glow-in-the-dark sense of peace and security. He is not asking us to deny ourselves fifty dollars to purchase "the tranquility of this beautiful platinum-plated cross."

Christ's cross is heavy, rough, with the smell of blood and death. But with its weight, burdens are lifted. With its bloody stains, souls are purified. With its splinters, consciences are pricked so we might to smoothed and shaped into his likeness. This deadly device brings new life!

They do make crosses like they used to in Spearfish, South Dakota.

A visitor to the famous Passion play there asked to see the cross after a performance. He was shocked at the weight. "I thought it would be hollow."

The actor portraying the Lord replied, "I must feel the weight of the cross to act like Christ."

Maybe they do make crosses like they used to.

22. Use the Power of "Three"

I'm not sure if it is some deep symbolism of the Trinity, but there is power in triplets. There's even research that indicates that groups of three are funnier than one or two. (There are not two or four "Stooges.")

Notice in the essay above, the use of triplets: "rugged, solid, durable"; "walnut, oak, or cherry"; "polished aluminum, Plexiglas, and fiberglass"; "sweat, blood, and drugged wine"; "blood, living water, and new wine"; and "heavy, rough, with the smell of blood and death."

Three is powerful!

5
KNOWING THE TECHNIQUES OF EFFECTIVE PERSUASION

Here are some actual attempts at "trying to persuade."

This [Christian] life is so great—I just love it whether it's true or not. (a televangelist's wife)

I find that theologians believe that unborn children and infants are saved because they have committed no personal sin. A popular book cites fetuses and infants inhabiting heaven. Therefore, why do evangelicals oppose abortion? Didn't abortion put more souls in heaven last year than Billy Graham? (letter to the editor in a national magazine)

If it was important for Jesus to visit Jerusalem several times a year, is it not important that you and your parishioners do the same at least once in a lifetime? (ad for a Holy Land tour)

These people have some serious trouble with logic! But God urges us, "Come now, let us reason together" (Isa. 1:18). The apostle Paul took this command seriously as he reasoned, explained, and proved the gospel of Christ. But how can we avoid what the apostle called "foolish and stupid arguments" (2 Tim. 2:23)?

MAKE A DISTINCTION BETWEEN "VALID" AND "ACCEPTABLE" ARGUMENTS

Valid Arguments

Valid arguments present an unavoidable conclusion based on the premise. If you agree with the evidence, you *must* accept the conclusion if you are a rational, intelligent thinker. The classic case argues (1) all men are mortal; (2) Socrates is a man; therefore, (3) Socrates is mortal.

If you agree that all humans are mortal and that Socrates is indeed a human, there is no other choice. Sooner or later, the famous philosopher was going to need a tombstone.

Acceptable Arguments

Acceptable arguments would consider that the conclusion of the illustration above is not unavoidable, but there's a *very* good chance that it *is* true. Acceptable arguments are based on statistics, laws of averages, precedents, habit, testimony, or scientific observation. Even science has few (if any) "valid" premises that are 100 percent conclusive. In fact, for something to be "probable" it only needs to be true a little more than half the time.

The following chart is used in scientific study to express "truthfulness."

1.0 Absolutely certain
.999–.901 Beyond reasonable doubt
.9 Highly probable
.899–.501 Probable
.5 Indifferent
.499–.101 Improbable

.1–.02 Highly improbable

.019–.001 False beyond reasonable doubt

0. Absolutely false

Most Christian doctrine fits into the "acceptable" category. (Wait! Before you organize a book burning, let me explain!) The arguments for the truthfulness of the Christian faith are based on *very, very reliable* evidence and observation. There are *excellent, rational* arguments. If the arguments were based on "valid" arguments, however, there would be no need for faith. Every rational human being would be forced by the indisputable evidence to know there is a God who must be worshipped.

In fact, almost all our assumptions in earthly living are based on acceptable, not valid, arguments. We act as if the law of averages will prevail and that scientific observation is reputable and reliable. We assume we will wake up in the same bed we fell asleep in, the kitchen will still be down the hall, our clothes will still be in the closet, safe drinking water will still come out of the faucet, our workplace will still be in the same location as yesterday at 5 p.m., and air will continue to contain adequate oxygen. Virtually everything we do is based on acceptable, but not valid, premises.

An earthquake or tornado *could* change everything we assumed would be true. The kitchen may now be in the next county. Even the classic "Socrates is mortal" breaks down when we take Elijah, who was taken up to eternity in the fiery chariot, into account. Only 99.9999999999 percent of people have been mortal, so this is not strictly a valid argument.

This is where faith comes into play. Scientists exercise faith in their instruments and their own powers of observation. There is always the chance that their readings and observations are inaccurate. As long as any premise is less than 100 percent, faith is required to act upon it. But as long as the observations or testimony are reliable, it is rational and reasonable to have faith—in science and in God.

But once we claim Christian doctrines are valid, unbelievers can tear our reasoning apart by *reducto ad absurdum.* This strategy disproves an argument by showing that at just one point, at just one time, it is contradictory or inconsistent. This distinction between valid and acceptable arguments, however, can work to the Christian's advantage. Haughty humanists need to realize that, by *faith,* they have determined "there is absolutely no absolute truth." Evolutionists need to be reminded that their "theory" requires faith to accept!

DEFINE THE TERMS OF DEBATE

Evolutionists and creationists have a difficult time debating the source of human life. Each side is certain their viewpoint is correct and that their opponent is wrong. To argue effectively, they must begin at a point where they both agree (or are at least open to the opposite view). Archaeological evidence of fossil records might be common ground to begin discussion. There must be common terms, words, and authority. Without common definitions, there can be no debate.

For instance, in ninth-grade debate class the issue was "Do UFOs exist?" Unfortunately, I ended up on the affirmative side. There were lots of books and theories, but nothing we felt would hold up in a debate. Finally we devised a plan. In just ten seconds we would prove the existence of unidentified flying objects.

I stood up to begin our presentation. Suddenly, from the back of the room, a friend lobbed a wad of aluminum foil at the panel. My partner quickly grabbed it and stuffed it under his coat.

"Do you know what that was?" I asked in my best prosecuting attorney voice. The negative team shrugged their shoulders in unison.

"Then you will agree that you could *not identify* it?" They nodded their heads.

"And will you agree that it did *fly* through the air?" Scowling, they nodded in agreement.

"And will you agree that it indeed was an *object?*" Heads reluctantly nodded a third time.

"Then you have just agreed that *unidentified flying objects* do exist."

Despite the high-pitched whining of "unfair," the debate was over because we had not previously defined terms or narrowly focused the subject. The debate topic should have read, "Proposed, that UFOs are piloted by intelligent life forms from another planet." Defining our terms is essential for effective persuasion.

USE SOURCES BOTH YOU AND YOUR AUDIENCE ACCEPT AS AUTHORITY

There are hundreds of examples of New Testament writers and characters appealing to the Old Testament. The Pharisees, Sadducees, and Temple leaders, while opposed to the teaching of Jesus and His disciples, did view the Old Testament as the final authority. The ancient Scriptures were the common ground to begin a persuasive presentation.

In evangelical and fundamentalist churches, sermons begin with Scripture because the majority of the congregation views it as an authority. However, in many churches and the vast majority of society, the Bible is simply a book of good teachings at best and fairy tales at worst. The Bible is not viewed as an acceptable authority.

Our culture rejects the concept of absolute truth, but evaluates truth by its relevance. That's why, as someone who has spoken at youth camps and conventions, I had to change my approach. I couldn't simply say, "The Bible says . . ." I had to build a case with anecdotes and examples—and occasionally throw in a major university study—of the various consequences of a particular action and *then* say, "That's why this biblical principle still works today." And, because the Bible *is* true, the benefits of following its moral principles are proven in university study after university study.

So, while we can't always use Scripture in our persuasion, we can use scientific studies, popular authors, music lyrics, philosophers, and so forth in our presentation. The apostle Paul even quoted ancient poets. For instance, here's number 7 in my "Top Ten Reasons I'm Not Divorcing My Wife." Rather than beginning with Malachi 2's condemnation of divorce, I make the case for why divorce is such a destructive act. (You can read the whole article at www.jameswatkins.com/divorce.htm.)

7. I'm not that crazy about dying prematurely.

I've spent too much time on my mountain bike being chased by dogs and eating fat-free (and taste-free) food to be killed off prematurely by a divorce.

According to a seventy-year prospective study reported in the *American Journal of Public Health* and the *American Psychologist*, divorce is comparable to two packs of cigarettes a day. Those divorced had a 40 percent greater risk of "premature death" than those who were steadily married. Men who remained single following a divorce fared even worse with a 120 percent greater chance of dying sooner. Women remaining single after divorce increase their risk by 80 percent.

And divorce can increase your chances of terminal cancer! That's what Dr. David B. Larson, president of the National Institute for Healthcare Research, claims following "extensive research." Divorced men were also found to be twice as likely to die of cardiovascular disease than their married counterparts. But wait, there's more. Larson found that three times more divorced people commit suicide than non-divorced.

That's why I'm going to exercise, eat right, and stay married! (And staying married is actually easier than jogging and eating oat bran.)

USE RELIABLE EVIDENCE

Not only must the authorities be accepted by both parties, but the evidence must be agreed upon as well. The conclusion (what the evidence *means*) is what is being argued. But the "link" is the crucial piece that takes your reader or listener from the evidence to the conclusion. Here's how it works: (1) the claim, (2) the evidence to support the claim, and (3) the link between the two.

Christ used this approach, called a "logical syllogism," when He was accused of casting out demons by the power of Satan: (1) "I am not of Satan" (the claim), (2) "A nation divided falls; a house divided falls" (the evidence that everyone would agree is true); (3) "Satan wouldn't work against himself" (the link that also is agreeable to both parties).

The link is the hinge pin that needs to firmly connect the evidence and claim together. There are many forms of evidence, such as the following:

Statistics

Numbers can be persuasive, but they can also be numbing. What is a trillion anyway? But there are effective ways to make numbers meaningful.

For instance, there have not been one trillion seconds since Christ was born! Or, how do you make the point that only 30 percent of teens will be retained by a local church? A creative youth sponsor lined up ten teens across the front of the church and begin reciting some recent studies. One by one, as the reasons for leaving the church were cited, teens began sitting down until only three were left. Those statistics made an impact—because the figures could be seen as real *people*, not just numbers. If you're going to use figures, put some flesh on them.

Statistics, however, have become suspect in recent years. The attitude seems to be summed up with "Figures don't lie, but liars figure."

Perhaps this point was best made by a former president's own budget man: "Nobody really knows what these figures mean." (He was quickly replaced in the administration.)

Here's another example. A chewing gum ad claimed that three out of four dentists surveyed recommended the brand for their patients who chewed gum. The ad gives the impression that all over America dentists are recommending this gum. I would like to know how *many* dentists were surveyed. All we can be sure of is four. Plus, the dentists *aren't* recommending you chew that particular gum, only to use it *if* you chew gum. And, let's be serious, how many patients go into the dentist's office and ask, "Doctor, what gum would you recommend?"

Narratives, Anecdotes

Chapter 9 is devoted to this subject.

Visuals

Again, the audience needs to be able to visualize the problem or solution. Graphs, photos, charts, cartoons, skits, demonstrations, role plays, or any way to *show* the solution will increase effectiveness and retention. (Psychologists claim we remember only 10 percent of what we hear, but 30 percent of what we see!)

Testimonies

Testimonies must be one of TV advertising's most effective methods. Just watch an infomercial with users gushing over how their lives have been changed forever using the "Super-Vege-Tron 2000" slicer and dicer.

To be credible, the person needs to be some kind of "expert" on the subject—whether a homemaker or professional chef—who actually has used the product. Lucy "I Love Lucy" Ricardo was *not* a credible spokesperson for the classic sitcom's fictitious "Vitameatavegamin."

Remember, though, the most reliable testimonies come from your opposition. (They have nothing to gain in arguments.) It was Christ's *enemies* who called Him "a man of integrity."

And, use only quotes that can be verified!

Compare/contrast

Right behind testimonials follow ads that claim products have 30 percent less fat, more active ingredients, are faster, cleaner, more powerful, less abrasive, sharper, less filling, lower in calories, better, or tastier.

Unfortunately, most ads only claim that "Brand X cleans better." Better than what? Better than dirt? It never claims to be better than "Brand Z"—just "better." "Brand Y" hot dogs have 30 percent less fat than *what*—a pound of lard?

Make sure you're comparing apples with apples, or oranges, or at least some member of the fruit family. Comparison/contrast evidence must *compare/contrast* with *something!*

Remember that the link that connects the evidence and the claim together is the key.

Knowing the techniques of effective persuasion is important—as well as the ineffective attempts we'll look at in the next chapter.

Don't have anything to do with foolish and stupid arguments.

2 Timothy 2:23

6

KNOWING THE TRAPS OF INEFFECTIVE PERSUASION

One of the most power tools of effective persuasion is to question your opponent's evidence or link. Christ and Paul certainly used this technique. "Jesus replied, 'You are in error because you do not know the Scriptures or the power of God'" (Matt. 22:29).

So we have divine precedent to question our opponent's logic. Paul was glad to report, "We have renounced secret and shameful ways; we do not use deception, nor do we distort the word of God. On the contrary, by setting forth the truth plainly we commend ourselves to every man's conscience in the sight of God" (2 Cor. 4:2–3). And Paul warns against "foolish and stupid arguments."

I've included some examples I have heard or read.

EITHER/OR

"You're either witnessing or you're not a Christian!"

Some things are black or white. One is either pregnant or not pregnant. We are "saved" or "lost." But in many areas, more than two options exist. We need to point out *other* options that exist if our opponents are incorrectly using the either/or argument.

LIMITING THE CONSEQUENCES

"If we don't offer a second worship service, our church won't grow."
The argument goes, "If A happens, then B and *only* B will occur."
This cousin to the either/or argument denies that other consequences are possible. There probably are.

FAULTY GENERALIZATIONS

"All those people at St. Mark's are liberals."

There is no evidence to support the claim. (Prejudice and bias, perhaps, but no evidence.) First, "all" should be avoided at all (OK, at *most*) costs. And "liberal" is such a general word that it has no meaning except for emotional connotations.

ILLUSTRATIONS AS PROOF

"Birds do not sow or reap or store away in barns, so why should Christians invest in Individual Retirement Accounts?"

Examples and illustrations do not *prove* anything. They only *illustrate*. And they can only depict one very narrow principle. If the writer is consistent, he must also move out of his house, build a nest, and eat worms!

Christ was not saying we should copy birds' behavior. They don't sow or reap because farmers do all the work for them. They don't store in barns because most fly to warmer climates in the winter months. Christ was saying, "If I can take care of the birds, I can take care of you."

Examples are powerful, but they don't prove anything. (We'll devote an entire chapter to the persuasive power of illustrations.)

BEGGING THE QUESTION

"God exists; His Word says so."

This argument only goes in circles. It tries to use the conclusion as the evidence. (If this book is outlawed, only outlaws will have this book.)

RED HERRINGS

Opposing teams in fox hunts would often drag a dead fish across, and then away from, the fox trail to confuse the dogs. Thus, "red herring" arguments attempt to avoid the real issue and get off on a tangent.

The apostle Paul used this to his advantage when appearing before the Jewish leaders:

> Then Paul, knowing that some of them were Sadducees and the others Pharisees, called out in the Sanhedrin, "My brothers, I am a Pharisee, the son of a Pharisee. I stand on trial because of my hope in the resurrection of the dead." When he said this, a dispute broke out between the Pharisees and the Sadducees, and the assembly was divided. (The Sadducees say that there is no resurrection, and that there are neither angels nor spirits, but the Pharisees acknowledge them all). (Acts 23:6–8)

LEADING QUESTIONS

Leading questions assume the answers. For instance, salespeople often ask, "Would you like the Rugs-R-Us Super Sucker 7000 delivered Monday or Tuesday?" but never "Do you want this vacuum cleaner?"

MISUSE OF LABELS

Some labels are so powerful that we can only see the name attached to that person. For instance: abortionist, atheist, conservative Christian, liberal, blue state, red state, right-winged radical, and so forth. Each of these words conjures up a stereotype that may not apply to the person at all. Be careful of labels that discredit individuals.

Labels can also disguise the truth. Vietnam was never a declared war, but a "police action." Nuclear missiles were known as "Peace Keepers." Supporters of abortion on demand are "pro choice."

Spiritual-sounding labels can also be abused. Have you noticed that the righteous don't worry, but are "burdened"? Anger becomes "righteous indignation." Sin is a "mistake" or "genetic disposition."

And "legalese" can intimidate and make the wisest people feel foolish as they read their loan contract. My will states that the executor must "dispose of remaining residue." Does that refer to taking out the trash or to disposing of *me*?

ONE INDIVIDUAL DOES NOT REPRESENT THE WHOLE

One danger is to assume that my experience should be everyone else's experience. "This is what God did in my life, so He must want to do that same thing in yours too." This is a real danger in a personal experience story.

Secondly, many times we assume guilt by association. If someone in an organization or group is proven to be unethical or immoral, that does not prove that everyone in that organization is unethical or immoral.

THE WHOLE DOES NOT REFLECT THE INDIVIDUAL MEMBERS

For instance many organizations are split several ways on key issues. To say one is a Republican or Democrat, United Methodist or Baptist, doesn't indicate his or her position on a specific issue.

FALSE STATEMENTS

Well-meaning Christians have spread some very misinformed information, such as the petitions that keep circulating warning that the FCC is planning to ban all religious broadcasting and the well-circulated rumor that Procter and Gamble is run by Satanists. We will lose any possibility of being persuasive if we are ill-informed or worse, misinformed.

Of course, when attacking an opponent's argument, we must never attack them personally. Paul warned in Colossians 4:5–6, "Be wise in the way you act toward outsiders; make the most of every opportunity. Let your conversation be always full of grace, seasoned with salt, so that you may know how to answer everyone."

The questions I constantly have to ask myself as I write my weekly newspaper column are these: *Is this column "full of grace"? Will this draw my opponents and "outsiders" closer to Jesus, or drive them further from Him?* Or to paraphrase 2 Corinthians 6:3, "We try to write in such a way that no one will be hindered from finding the Lord by the way we write."

PART 2
CHANGING
LIVES WITH
INTENSITY

Serve [God] with wholehearted devotion and
with a willing mind, for the Lord searches
every heart and understands every motive
behind the thoughts.
1 Chronicles 28:9

7

USING
PSYCHOLOGICAL
APPEALS

n chapter 1, I mentioned the importance of having specific goals for our writing, specifically what we want our readers to know, feel, and do. As I worked with developing curriculum for senior high students, I began to doubt the effectiveness in changing behavior with the traditional model *message changes attitude—attitude changes behavior.*

There seemed to be a breakdown in that students could *know* something, even *feel* something, and then walk out of class and *do* the exact opposite. And the breakdown was not limited to senior high Sunday school. Pastors could preach powerful sermons on Sunday, but Monday, there was no appreciable difference in parishioners' lives.

THEORIES OF CHANGE

So, how does one go about changing attitude and behaviors, and thus lives? There are several theories. Daryl J. Bem in his book, *Beliefs, Attitudes, and Human Affairs*, analyzes some of the more popular theories.

Cognitive Theories

Cognitive theories derive from the word *cognition*, which means the conscious process of the mind by which individuals perceive, think, and remember. If we can change a person's thinking, we can change his or her behavior. That's the traditional Sunday school and church model and was affirmed by academia in Carl Hovland's "Yale Attitude Change Approach": Change thinking and you change behavior.

In applying this to writing and speaking, one would simply present the facts, as many scriptures imply:

"Then you will know the truth, and the truth will set you free." (John 8:32)

Then Peter stood up with the Eleven, raised his voice and addressed the crowd: "Fellow Jews and all of you who live in Jerusalem, let me explain this to you; listen carefully to what I say. . . ."

When the people heard this, they were cut to the heart and said to Peter and the other apostles, "Brothers, what shall we do?" (Acts 2:14, 37)

How, then, can they call on the one they have not believed in? And how can they believe in the one of whom they have not heard? And how can they hear without someone preaching to them? And how can they preach unless they are sent? As it is written, "How beautiful are the feet of those who bring good news!" (Rom. 10:14–15)

Social Construct Theories

Kurt Lewin, of the University of Michigan, argued that contrary to the Yale Attitude Change Theory, persuasion occurs, not simply by receiving a persuasive message, but by depending on others for knowledge about the world and even about oneself. He called this the "Group Dynamics Theory." Bem referred to it as "nonconscious ideology," arguing that beliefs and attitudes were taught by a person's "reference group" of family, friends, and society as a whole.

Another theory argues that "collective socially-constructed realities" (don't you love these pompous, academic terms?) such as family, friends, teachers, and peers unconsciously—and irresistibly—form our values and beliefs.

Bem argued that, despite our claims of individual critical thinking, we are more susceptible to the mass media than we would like to think. But even more powerful than the media is interpersonal influence and societal norms. The author concluded,

> Nearly every group to which we belong, from our immediate families to our societies as a whole, has an implicit or explicit set of beliefs, attitudes, and behaviors which are considered appropriate for its members. Any member of a group who strays from those norms risks isolation and social disapproval; in other words, groups regulate beliefs, attitudes, and behaviors through the use of social reward and punishment. ("Beliefs, Attitudes, and Human Affairs," *Basic Concepts in Psychology*.)

Others call it "Referential Persuasion" in that the subject is persuaded, not necessarily by the persuader, but by the reactions of those around them that respect to the persuader. The message is legitimized by peers.

In a study of an election in Ann Arbor, Michigan, S. J. Eldersveld and R. W. Dodge studied the effects of three groups on voters. One group personally visited voters to discuss the benefits of the proposed legislation. One group received four mailings in favor of the legislations. And one group was exposed to only broadcast and print media's support of the legislation.

Of those personally visited, 75 percent voted in favor of the legislation. Of those receiving the mailings, 45 percent voted in favor. And of those exposed to only media, 19 percent voted in favor of the legislation.

Which raises the important question, Why am I wasting my time writing books and newspaper columns?! And why are you wasting your time reading this book?

E. Katz observed that any effect of the media is a "two-step flow of communication." Media may influence "opinion leaders," but "rank and file" are influenced by what the "opinion leaders" say — not what the media says directly. Katz's model, then, is *media changes attitude/behavior of "opinion leader"; opinion leader changes attitude/behavior of rank and file.*

So, that's why I'm writing a book aimed at the opinion leaders — writers and speakers. Our audience may not be the person in the pew, but the person in the pulpit or public office.

Scripture documents how peers and powerful leaders provide a persuasive effect:

> They devoted themselves to the apostles' teaching and to the fellowship, to the breaking of bread and to prayer. Everyone was filled with awe, and many wonders and miraculous signs were done by the apostles. . . . Every day they continued to meet together in the temple courts. They broke bread in their homes and ate together with glad and sincere hearts, praising God and enjoying the favor of all the people. And the Lord added to their number daily those who were being saved. (Acts 2:42–43, 46–47)

> I am not writing this to shame you, but to warn you, as my dear children. Even though you have ten thousand guardians in Christ, you do not have many fathers, for in Christ Jesus I became your father through the gospel. Therefore I urge you to imitate me. (1 Cor. 4:14–16)

Behavioral Theories

Bem also explored behavioral or "Pavlovian conditioning" on our attitudes and beliefs. (Remember Pavlov's dog that associated food with the sound of bell, so when the bell rang, the dog began to salivate—even if there was no food in sight.)

Bem quoted a study by Arthur and Carolyn Starrts on the development of racial prejudice that claimed that attitudes toward various nationalities were "learned" through classical conditioning.

Bem also quoted studies that show that what a person believes he or she feels about a certain stimuli can be manipulated by feedback from peers. In fact, the author argued we don't know what we're feeling until someone tells us what we're feeling!

To prove his point, Bem described an experiment by Stanley Schachter and Jerome Singer. Subjects were injected with adrenalin and then placed in a room with an accomplice working for the doctors. When the accomplice appeared angry, the subjects claimed the drug made them feel angry as well. When the accomplice appeared euphoric, the subjects reported the drug made them feel euphoric.

Bem directly challenged "the common assumption that one cannot change the behavior of men until one has changed their 'hearts and minds' first." The author argued that behavior must first be changed for the heart and mind to be changed.

One could imply this from Romans 12.

And so, dear brothers and sisters, I plead with you to give your bodies to God. . . . Let them be a living and holy sacrifice—the kind he will find acceptable. This is truly the way to worship him. Don't copy the behavior and customs of this world, but let God transform you into a new person by changing the way you think. *Then* you will learn to know God's will for you, which is good and pleasing and perfect. (Rom. 12:1–2 NLT, emphasis added)

Thus, *behavior* changes attitudes and beliefs. Could this be why the church has become so ineffective in changing society?

According to a George Barna study, so-called Christians exhibit virtually no difference from non-Christians in their lifestyles. "Desiring to have a close, personal relationship with God" ranks sixth among the twenty-one life goals tested among "born-again" believers, trailing such desires as "living a comfortable lifestyle." Twenty-five percent of non-Christians engage in premarital sex, compared to 24 percent for Christians, making them statistically identical. Thirty-seven percent of pastors admit to sexually inappropriate behavior with parishioners. And, on a somewhat related topic, "born again" church members are more likely to get divorced than non-church members! (Some 25 percent of all adults have been divorced, but 29 percent of Baptists and 34 percent of non-denominational church members have divorced. Mainline churches had a similar rate to the general public.)

All the preaching on the Ten Commandments seems undercut by the behavioral example in the pulpit and pews. This creates some serious cognitive dissonance and seems to make the case for the next theory.

Cognitive Dissonance Theories

Leon Festinger was first to coin the term "Cognitive Dissonance Theory" as he observed that people cannot tolerate discrepancy between their own and other similar people's attitudes as well as tension within the individual's own cognitive system.

Using this theory, Bem argued, "If an individual is induced to engage in behavior that is inconsistent with his beliefs or attitudes, he will experience the discomfort of 'cognitive dissonance,' which will motivate him to seek a resolution of that inconsistency."

Fritz Heider called it "Balance Theory" in that people prefer emotional and mental balance as opposed to unbalance. It is called "Congruency Theory" by T. M. Newcomb, who observed that individuals tend to feel most comfortable when their beliefs, attitudes, and actions are all in homeostasis or harmony with each other.

The classic biblical example is Paul in Romans 7:

> So I find this law at work: When I want to do good, evil is right there with me. For in my inner being I delight in God's law; but I see another law at work in the members of my body, waging war against the law of my mind and making me a prisoner of the law of sin at work within my members. What a wretched man I am! Who will rescue me from this body of death? (Rom. 7:21–24)

This caused him to make a dramatic change in his life:

> Those who live according to the sinful nature have their minds set on what that nature desires; but those who live in accordance with the Spirit have their minds set on what the Spirit desires. The mind of sinful man is death, but the mind controlled by the Spirit is life and peace; the sinful mind is hostile to God. It does not submit to God's law, nor can it do so. Those controlled by the sinful nature cannot please God.

> You, however, are controlled not by the sinful nature but by the Spirit, if the Spirit of God lives in you. And if anyone does not have the Spirit of Christ, he does not belong to Christ. But if Christ is in you, your body is dead because of sin, yet your spirit is alive because of righteousness. (Rom. 8:5–8)

We must be careful in applying balance theories, however. Imagine I'm a millionaire. I'm sitting through a sermon that emphasizes Christ's command to look out for the well-being of the poor. Prior to coming to church, I evicted a single mom and her three children because she was a week late in her rent. Earlier that week I had foreclosed on a struggling business. And at Christmas, I refused to allow the Salvation Army to have a red kettle outside my office building.

Suddenly, there is "cognitive dissonance" in my soul. To resolve that conflict, I can do one of four things:

1. *Defame the messenger.* "The preacher is a bleeding-heart liberal who wants to tax me to death. He's jealous that I have what, in the dark recesses of his soul, he wants but can't have."

2. *Discount the message.* "He's taking Scripture out of context. Christ was speaking to another culture, so this doesn't apply to me today."

3. *Distort the message.* "What he's really talking about is how the bleeding-heart liberals in Congress want to tax me to death. And when they tax me to death, I can't give a hundred dollars to the local rescue mission each year."

4. *Demonstrate the message.* "I've been acting like a sinful Scrooge. I'm going to go to that single mom and apologize for evicting them and give them some extra time to pay. I'm going to give a generous donation to the Salvation Army and invite them to ring their bells outside of all my businesses. Plus, I need to evaluate my lifestyle."

Until I have acted on *one* of those options, I am filled with emotional anxiety. And humans cannot live long with anxiety.

This anxiety can also be the result of positive pressure. Imagine, again, I'm that millionaire with a twenty-room mansion with an indoor pool and racquetball court. I have three Mercedes in my four-car garage (the fourth is a Lamborghini). And I'm planning to spend the summer on the Mediterranean.

I pick up a book that claims "Only Christ can offer real love, joy, and peace." Prior to picking it up, I've been feeling depressed because all my material things haven't provided the satisfaction I thought they would. Maybe it's because I just lost a million or two in the stock market. If I can just close that deal with GM, I think I'll be happy.

Again, there is that dissonance in my soul that must be relieved. (In the next chapter, we'll discuss how humor can reveal incongruity—in a nonthreatening way—in the reader and listener's life.)

We must be careful that we don't alienate our readers with too much pressure, or their natural instinct will be to defame the messenger, discount the message, or distort the message.

And we must also be aware of the problem of "ego involvement." The more personally invested I am in an issue, the harder I will be to persuade. This may be why Christ warned,

> "I tell you the truth, it is hard for a rich man to enter the kingdom of heaven. Again I tell you, it is easier for a camel to go through the eye of a needle than for a rich man to enter the kingdom of God."
>
> When the disciples heard this, they were greatly astonished and asked, "Who then can be saved?"
>
> Jesus looked at them and said, "With man this is impossible, but with God all things are possible." (Matt. 19:23–26)

"Cognitive complexity" is another challenge. A professor in grad school described it best with the question "How many holes do you have in your pasta maker?" If I am a rigid legalist, I may have only two holes in my mental pasta maker: black and white. (In psychology, these people are diagnosed as having "borderline personalities.") A "gray" message cannot be accepted, but will be forced through either the black or white hole. There is no gray hole; *everything* is black or white. The fewer the holes in the pasta maker, the harder to accept a new option or alternative in thinking.

However, if I have more of a sieve than a pasta maker, I will accept any and all options. We see this in the attitude that there are no absolutes, everything is relative. In India, for instance, I found it very hard to share my faith in Christ. "Oh, Jesus," they would reply. "He is one of our favorite gods." In today's culture, the problem is too many holes in the pasta maker!

NO ONE THEORY IS SUFFICIENT

Each theory has validity, but it is more likely that we are influenced by *all* sources from head knowledge to modeling of social behavior. Bem wrote, "A man's beliefs and attitudes have their foundation in four human activities: thinking, feeling, behaving, and interacting with others."

Think of each theory, then, as a tool. Obviously a variety of tools may be necessary to complete a home repair project. Hammers work well for pounding nails but are less effective in driving screws. One would be hard pressed, however, to drive nails with a screwdriver. (And, in most cases, one would not use a screwdriver and hammer simultaneously.)

In the same way, various cognitive, affective, and behavioral tools may all be needed to complete a persuasive project. This of course, is humbling to writers who believe their words alone can make a significant change. It underscores the need for divine help in the process of changing hearts and minds.

[Jesus said,] "When he, the Spirit of truth, comes, he will guide you into all truth." (John 16:13)

My message and my preaching were not with wise and persuasive words, but with a demonstration of the Spirit's power, so that your faith might not rest on men's wisdom, but on God's power. (1 Cor. 2:4–5)

This is what we speak, not in words taught us by human wisdom but in words taught by the Spirit, expressing spiritual truths in spiritual words. The man without the Spirit does not accept the things that come from the Spirit of God, for they are foolishness to him, and he cannot understand them, because they are spiritually discerned. (1 Cor. 2:13–14)

You yourselves are our letter, written on our hearts, known and read by everybody. You show that you are a letter from Christ, the result of our ministry, written not with ink but with the Spirit of the living God, not on tablets of stone but on tablets of human hearts. (2 Cor. 3:2–3)

CHANGE IS OFTEN INCREMENTAL

Ministers love the story of Saul of Tarsus' miraculous transformation into the apostle Paul. It was nearly an instant 0 to 10 transformation from persecutor of Christians to preacher of Christ! Unfortunately this Damascus Road experience is not typical. More often it's Nicodemus who comes to Jesus by night (John 3). No immediate decision or change occurs. In fact we find him next, along with other religious leaders, questioning Jesus' teachings in John 7. It is not until John 19:39—twelve chapters later—that we see Nicodemus again, this time helping Joseph of Arimathea prepare Christ's body for burial. At what point did Nicodemus decide to follow Jesus? Was it a number of steps from 0 to 3, 3 to 7, 7 to 10?

Most people change incrementally—perhaps one or two steps at a time. Jesus seemed to imply this as He used the examples of seeds, vines, and branches for spiritual change and growth. You don't plant a mustard *seed* on Tuesday and expect to find a mustard *tree* on Wednesday. It's often slow growth.

If our audience is at a 2 spiritually, perhaps we should urge them to move to a 3 or 5. They are probably not ready for a 9 or 10. Yes, there are people who dramatically, miraculously leap from 1 to 10. And 10 should always be the goal. But most people change incrementally.

For example, instead of urging the abolition of abortion, perhaps we should urge abstinence-based sexual education, parental notification laws, and more encouragement to keep babies (and provide the resources necessary for a poor woman to do that). Let the record show I'd like to see abortion completely disappear from our world, but I'm practical enough to realize the change will probably come in baby steps.

Communicating to change lives is a long, and at times, frustrating process. But don't become discouraged by a lack of immediate, dramatic results. It took nearly two hundred years to eliminate slavery in the United States, but the faithful, persistent writing and speaking of abolitionists eventually prevailed. If you're writing for a godly cause, you too will prevail, but probably not by next Thursday!

[Jesus said,] "You blind guides! You
strain out a gnat but swallow a camel."
Matthew 23:24

8
USING HUMOR
AS A PERSUASIVE
TOOL

Jesus was a standup comedian. Really!

The hip humor in first-century Palestine was hyperbole or intentional exaggeration. So when Jesus told the Pharisees, "You blind guides! You strain out a gnat but swallow a camel," He had the non-Pharisees rolling on the hillsides. He spoke of looking for a speck of sawdust in a person's eye while having a log in your own. Jesus also pointed out that the rich getting into heaven was as challenging as pulling a camel through the eye of a needle. (Preachers have ruined the story by imagining a short, narrow gate called "the needle's eye," which required point one, the camel had to get down on its knees; point two, someone had to unload all the baggage on its back; point three we, too, must take off the material baggage and kneel at the cross for salvation. No, Jesus was talking about *real* camels and *real* needles' eyes to get a laugh and make a powerful point.)

Jesus also used ridiculous—and humorous—situations. Today, hiding a lamp under a bed draws no laughter, but in first-century Palestine it did. A lamp was an open flame and a bed was a flat, dry grass mat. The lamp would not be hidden long!

Effective Christian communicators have often used humor. When someone scolded Charles Spurgeon for using humor in his sermons, the late, great preacher answered, "This preacher thinks it less of a crime to cause a momentary laughter than a half hour of profound slumber."

Likewise, famous Christian journalist G. K. Chesterton wrote, "I am all in favor of laughing. Laughing has something in it in common with the ancient words of faith and inspiration; it unfreezes pride and unwinds secrecy; it makes men forget themselves in the presence of something greater than themselves."

Recently, scientific research has been conducted on the effectiveness of humor in persuasive messages. A "scientific study of humor" sounds as much an oxymoron as jumbo shrimp, airline food, or government intelligence, but I actually wrote a paper in graduate school called "Effectiveness of the Use of Humor on Persuasive Messages in Print." Here are some of those findings.

THE SCIENCE OF HUMOR

Yes, your tax dollars have actually paid for nearly one hundred government funded studies of humor.

In 1972, Goldstein and McGhee broke humor into three categories: aggressive (the Three Stooges, the Roadrunner), sexual, and nonsense. Kelly and Solomon, in 1975, divided humor into seven categories: puns, understatements, jokes, ludicrous situations, satire, irony, and finally, humorous intent. However, my informal study of late night and Internet humor breaks down to three: rude, crude, and lewd.

No matter how you divide it up, university studies have shown that humor attracts attention in all types of persuasive messages. Humor does not enhance source credibility, but it does increase likeability. (People love clowns, but don't elect them to office. OK, bad example.) According to a 1990 study by Biel and Brigwater, individuals who liked an advertisement were twice as likely to be persuaded to act upon it. And a 1980 study showed that textbooks that used relevant humor were most liked by students. Yes, humor improves comprehension in education.

Also in 1990, Gortham and Christophel set up an experiment in "Introduction to Statistics" classes. (Now there's a coma-inducing subject!) Two classes were taught by the same professor, but in one class relevant humor was used and the other class included no humor. Researchers found that in the class using humor, students scored 10 percent higher than their counterparts. Earlier studies by Zillman and Vance had found the same results in five- to seven-year-olds.

Humor Increases Attention, Comprehension, and Retention of Information

But humor alone is not effective in changing attitudes and behavior. There is solid proof that humor increases attention, comprehension, and retention, but it may or may not be effective in actual persuasion and action steps. Notice in the gospels that Jesus used humorous illustrations (straining out gnats and swallowing camels) but then followed up with a deadly serious point.

Humor can be used effectively to get attention, comprehension, and retention, but it also causes the listener or reader to lower his or her defenses. Think of humor as "laughing gas" that allows you to drill away at sensitive subjects.

Humor Connects with Readers

According to William Frye at Stanford University, as you laugh, your body produces endorphins. These are natural chemicals that stimulate circulation, respiration, the central nervous system, and the immune system. They also serve as natural pain relievers. The minimum daily adult requirement, according to the studies, is fifteen laughs per day, three of which must be "belly" laughs. Using humor, then, literally creates good feelings in our readers and listeners.

Equally powerful in humor is the awareness of "I've felt that same way" or "That happens to my family all the time." The best sitcoms and standup routines are funny because we see ourselves (or most often others) in the humorous situation. It brings a sense of connection. We have something in common, even if only our eccentric uncles.

Here's an excerpt from a column that definitely connected with women.

MEN ARE DIRT

My wife and I can't agree on the definition of "clean."

For instance, I think that cleaning up 99.9 percent of my mustache trimmings from the bathroom sink should earn an "A" for cleanliness. No! One whisker is a D-! And the same for the bathroom mirror. Considering the entire surface area of the mirror (8 square meters), one spot of toothpaste/saliva mixture (0.5 centimeter) would constitute a cleanliness quotient of 99.9999999999. We won't even go into my favorite mug, which Lois is convinced is the source of the West Nile Virus, the recent anthrax scare, and a possible Ebola outbreak. I think the mug simply has character after several uses.

I suppose it all goes back to Adam and Eve.

"And the Lord God formed man of the dust of the ground, and breathed into his nostrils the breath of life; and man became a living soul. And the Lord God caused a deep sleep to fall upon Adam, and he slept: and he took one of his ribs, and closed up the flesh instead thereof; And the rib, which the Lord God had taken from man, made he a woman, and brought her unto the man."

Simply put, man was created from dirt, while woman was created in some kind of sophisticated surgical procedure involving genetic engineering.

Thus, there is an inbred instinct that draws boys (of all ages) and dirt together.

This is easily explained by the old law of physics that "nature abhors a vacuum." This law is proven regularly on my desktop. As soon as I have it cleared off, it will attract all kinds of clutter from far reaches of the cosmos (paper clips, Post-Its, Kleenex, junk mail, magazines, coupons, stacks of reference books, computer disks, pens without ink and pencils with broken leads, plus reams of paper covered by a thin layer of preformed man). This will continue until the maximum clutter capacity is reached.

In the same way, by cleaning off a five-year-old boy, you are tampering with the forces of nature. This squeaky clean vacuum—that is bathed and dressed in his Sunday best—must be immediately equalized with a like amount of dirt! It's simple physics!

Anyway, here's my theory: Men simply take a more scientific, even metaphysical approach to dirt.

There's more, but you get the idea.

Humor Comforts Our Readers

Best-selling humorist Barbara Johnson is a prime example of the concept that "comedy is tragedy plus time" (someday we're going to laugh about it). Barbara has experienced more pain and loss than most spouses or parents, and yet she is able to write with wit and humor. Our shared experience, told in a witty rather than whining manner, comforts.

The apostle Paul wrote, ". . . we can comfort those in any trouble with the comfort we ourselves have received from God" (see 2 Cor.

1:1–4). "A cheerful heart" is indeed good medicine (Prov. 17:22). And so, if you're going to age, at least age with humor.

EIGHT PILL BOTTLES OLD

You can tell the age of a tree by counting the rings on the trunk. You can count horses' teeth. Scientists can even date rock and Strom Thurman with carbon dating. And, here's my theory: you can tell a person's age by counting the pills in his or her medicine cabinet.

Between ages one and sixteen, my one pill a day was Flintstones' chewable vitamins. Actually, I started out on something akin to Lucy's "Vitameatavegamin." Each morning, my mom would tackle me, pin me to the floor, and force a tablespoon of Vit-a-Gag-a-Choke-a-Retch down my throat. Thank goodness for Fred, Wilma, Barney, and Betty! So, one pill bottle: one to sixteen years old.

At sixteen, my hormones waged war against my body and suddenly my face erupted into full-scale, thermonuclear acne. Add to the battle-scarred landscape 1970-style braces, and it looked like Paris had been bombed with the Eiffel Tower lying in ruins across the destruction. Fortunately, there were tetracycline pills, which brought a bit of peace to my war-ravaged face. So, two pill bottles: sixteen to twenty years old.

In my twenties, I discovered I had inherited my mother and grandmother's arthritis in my neck and fingers. My grandmother's fingers were so twisted she could pull the cork from a wine bottle with her pinkie. So, I added Extra-Strength Bufferin to the medicine cabinet. So, three pill bottles: twenty years old.

When I hit thirty, cholesterol was the medical menace du jour, so I had it checked and discovered mine was 307. That's roughly the number for a three-hundred-pound couch potato whose diet consists solely of pork rinds and deep-fat-fried Twinkies. Since I weighed 150, rode bike, and tried to eat right, I was prescribed Lipitor, and my cholesterol promptly dropped to 200. Now, four pill bottles: thirty years old.

At forty-five I now was taking a multi-vitamin with 3000 percent of the daily adult requirement of the entire alphabet (A–zinc), Vitamin C to keep from catching colds, Ibuprofen for arthritis, glucosamine chondroitin to keep my fingers from turning into corkscrews, a regular aspirin to prevent heart attacks, Lipitor to keep my cholesterol under the deep-fat-fried Twinkie level, and Zyrtec for living in northern Indiana: the pollen capital of North America. So, seven bottles: forty-five years old.

But it's gotten worse at fifty. I now take Welbutrin to keep from getting depressed about all the pill bottles in our medicine cabinet. Between my wife and me, we have a pill *drawer* and, here's the worst: I bought one of those pillboxes with the days of the week on each compartment! I might as well tattoo GEEZER across my forehead! So, eight different pills a day: fifty years old.

At seventy, my mom has more drugs in her kitchen cabinet than a meth dealer! She now buys her over-the-counter meds at Sam's Club in the economical fifty-five-gallon drum.

And, if you watch the evening news, you know it only gets worse: pills for impotence, incontinence, heart attacks, blood clots, gas, bloating, indigestion, hot flashes, feminine dryness, cramping, the forgetfulness of Alzheimer's, and, well, I can't remember the rest. And have you noticed all those ads where the super-absorbent material always soaks up *blue* liquid. Blue body fluids?! That can't be healthy!

So, here's my theory: One pill a day, you're ready for kindergarten.

Two to three pills a day, high school and college.

Four to five pills, it's time to move out of your parents' house.

Six to nine, you're eligible to join AARP and Medicare.

More than ten pill bottles, you're old enough for carbon dating.

But I *am* grateful for my anti-allergy, anti-blood clot, anti-cho-
lesterol, anti-inflammation, and anti-depression drugs. Without
them, my arteries would be clogged like a Drano ad and I'd be sitting in the dark writing poetry about pain, death, and postnasal drip.
Worse, someone else's byline would have been on this column
years ago!

Now, if you'll excuse me, with all the stress of trying to make
my deadline with Internet problems, I need my Prilosec OTC pill.

Arrrgh! That's *nine*!

Humor Confronts Our Readers

Christ used humor to reveal His listeners' inconsistencies. German
philosopher Arthur Schopenhauer claimed that laughter is the "sudden
perception of incongruity" between our ideals and our behavior.

As mentioned earlier, humor is the laughing gas that keeps the
reader in the chair as we drill away on sensitive subjects. Here's an
example from my September 1997 newspaper column:

I'm coming out of the politically correct closet and announcing
to the world, "Yep! I'm intolerant!"

For instance, do you really want to go to an "open-minded" doctor with signs in the waiting room that read "I Brake for Bacteria";
"Save the Salmonella"; "Take a Stand for Polio"? I want a doctor
who is narrow-minded and completely intolerant to disease and
physical afflictions when I'm told, "Turn your head and cough."

And I'm *not* getting on a plane with a pilot who comes over the
intercom with "Welcome aboard Lame Duck Airlines. We'll be
traveling at whatever speed and altitude feels good at the time and
should be arriving at our destination in time for happy hour. So, put
your seat in recline position, hold on tight to your carry-ons, and
we'll be ready for take-off as soon as we cut off that 747 on our way

to the runway." (Where did he say the emergency exits were?!)

How about a tolerant mechanic at the brake shop? "I don't like to use the words 'safe' or 'unsafe' when it comes to brake shoes. I prefer to think of them having mechanical diversity."

Or a tolerant math teacher? "Well, Johnny, if 2 + 2 is 5 for you, then I'm not going to put any moral judgments on your mathematical worldview."

I don't even want to think about tolerant parachute packers, nuclear power plant operators, or driver's ed teachers ("Stop signs are arbitrary restrictions on our personal freedom").

Most of all, I'm downright intolerant when it comes to my kids. If I really love them, I'm going to be narrow-minded toward anything that is harmful to their physical, mental, social, and spiritual well-being. That's why I'm judgmental toward plaque buildup, kiddy porn, gangs, strep throat, "put-downs," undercooked hamburgers, spaced-out cults, illegal drugs, and nicotine (tobacco execs are simply serial killers in suits).

You're welcomed to be tolerant of this column. You can tape it to your refrigerator or use it to housebreak your new puppy. Somehow civilization will manage to continue despite your judgment of my writing.

But I'm not so sure that our society will continue if "Thou shalt not be intolerant" becomes the eleventh commandment. Perhaps we could be a bit more narrow-minded in observing the first ten.

FINDING HUMOROUS MATERIAL

Any time I share this material at a conference, inevitably someone—usually with a pocket protector filled with engineering pens—objects by saying, "But I'm not a funny person." I believe humor is a way of looking at life just a degree or two from normal.

Don't Take Life Too Seriously

Greek theater was divided into two categories: tragedies and comedies. Tragic tales had dire endings, such as the bountiful body counts at the end of many Shakespeare's plays. In comedies, however, the hero and heroine always lived "happily ever after" or at least had a pulse at the curtain call.

Romans 8:28 provides the ultimate punch line: "And we know that in all things God works for the good of those who love him, who have been called according to his purpose."

So, life is sort of a good news/bad news joke. The bad news, my wife nearly died giving birth to our first child, so she spent five days in intensive care and we had few maternity benefits with our insurance. The good news, all the expenses became "major medical" and every bill was paid by the insurance company. The bad news, it took three surgeries to remove my stubborn kidney stone. The good news, I still get fan mail from the column I wrote on my medical misadventures. The bad news, I forgot to put oil in our new car—ever—and the engine burned up, costing us $4,129 to replace. OK, I haven't seen the good in that!

As Christians, we have Romans 8:28 as the ultimate punch line, so we can at least be consoled that someday our situation will make a great anecdote for an article or talk. That's why I remind writers, "Nothing terrible happens to authors, just terrific anecdotes."

Don't Take Your Senses Too Seriously

Christ reminds us that "If your eyes are good, your whole body will be full of light. But if your eyes are bad, your whole body will be full of darkness" (Matt. 6:22–23). In other words, how we look at things determines our actions and attitudes. Some people simply refuse to see the humor in situations; their lives are filled with a dark seriousness. But a sense of humor can be developed. It can see beyond sight, hearing, touch, taste, and smell to detect all the interesting surprises, inconsistencies, and contradictions others can't sense.

For instance, while in a desperate struggle with an "easy to install" shelving unit, I asked my then five-year-old son to get me the yardstick. Five minutes—and one migraine—later, I heard scraping and rustling down the hallway. I turned to see Paul dragging half a tree.

"Paul, what are you doing?! I said I needed a yardstick."

"But, Dad,"—he looked at me innocently—"this was the biggest stick in the yard."

I let the shelving unit collapse and had an endorphin-producing belly laugh as I hugged my son.

A large part of humor is looking at life from a fresh, slightly different perspective—even our faith. Flannery O'Connor wrote that Christianity is serious business that creates serious comedy. "Only if we are secure in our beliefs, can we see the comical side of the universe."

Don't Take Yourself Too Seriously

Obviously, not everything in life is funny. We need to take our faith and friendships seriously. But Proverbs 17:22 not only observes that "a cheerful heart is a good medicine," but warns "a crushed spirit dries up the bones."

It takes an incredible amount of time and energy to keep up a serious and dignified front, but the unbearable pressure to perform perfectly squeezes the life—and humor—out of a person. There is a deep-down joy—and confidence in God's control—that allows Christians a real reason to laugh. That's why Conrad Hyers wrote, "Humor is not the opposite of seriousness. Humor is the opposite of despair."

And once we've learned to laugh at ourselves, we have a lifetime of humorous material.

CAUTIONS FOR WRITING WITH HUMOR

Humor is a two-edged light saber: It can be used for both the light and dark side.

Use Humor to Help, Not Hurt

As I mentioned earlier, most late-night and Internet humor seems to be rude, crude, and lewd. While Christ used irony, satire, paradox, and hyperbole, we find only one case of sarcasm: Matthew 23.

Use Humor to Introduce or Reinforce a Point

Humor used simply to get your readers' attention, or to keep them awake between points nine and ten, merely distracts from the point we're trying to make. Ideally, when readers remember the humor, they remember the message.

Use Humor Discreetly, Tastefully

Know your audience's sensitivities. And never, ever, use ethnic, racist, or sexist humor. This doesn't mean you can't use humor with sensitive subjects. I signed a contract and cashed the advance on a book about death for teenagers. Then, the editor called to say, "Oh, I forgot to mention, use lots of humor so the book isn't too depressing." What?! Humor in a book about death?! With much fear and trembling, I began each chapter with some, what I hoped was, appropriate humor, such as this chapter on grief.

No one seems to "die" in our culture. They've simply been called home, given up the ghost, returned to dust, gone the way of all mortal flesh, flown to their heavenly reward, crossed over the Jordan, traveled on to Glory, moved upstairs to sing in the heavenly choir.

The less religious are said to be on ice, six feet under, pushing up daisies, and shoveling coal. Their meter has expired. They've breathed their last, met the Grim Reaper, keeled over, bit the big one, kicked the bucket, bought the farm, cashed in their chips, closed up shop, made the final deadline, went home feet first, shuffled off to Buffalo, and brought down the final curtain. The fat lady has sung, and Elvis has left the building.

Actually, they're D-E-A-D!

Funeral director Jim Stone says, "One of the most important reasons for a funeral is to help the family and friends realize that their loved one has 'died.' Christians do have the hope that the one they love 'has gone to his eternal reward,' but as a funeral director I must help them cope with the fact that the earthly relationship is over."

Use Humor Sparingly

Remember my story of misunderstanding that the spaghetti sauce recipe called for *chopped* garlic rather than *powdered* garlic. Lightly sprinkle humor throughout the manuscript.

SECRETS OF WRITING HUMOR

Here are some suggestions:

Put the Punch Line Last

This sounds so obvious, but I need to be aware of that with each new column. For instance, which is more humorous?

I'm critically acclaimed but commercially ashamed since my books have won awards, but never a spot on the best-sellers lists.

My books have won awards, but never a spot on the best-sellers lists. I'm critically acclaimed but commercially ashamed.

Correct! The second.

Use Details

Have you ever tried to share something funny that happened at school or work with family and friends, and they just didn't get it? You reply, "You just had to be there." Your task as a writer or speaker is to take them there with all the necessary details that set up the punch line.

Work on Your Timing

Be sure you read your article or chapter aloud. Better yet, have someone in your writers' group read it aloud to the group. Did you take too long to get to the punch line? Was it rushed? Like face-to-face comedy, timing in writing is the secret.

Read Other Humorists

You can't get any better than Dave Barry and Irma Bombeck. Notice how they set up jokes, surprise you with the unexpected, and tap into your own fears and foibles.

Finally, this encouragement from Mary Hirsh: "Humor is a rubber sword. It allows you to make a point without drawing blood."

Jesus spoke all these things to the crowd in parables; he did not say anything to them without using a parable.

Matthew 13:34

9
USING STORIES, ILLUSTRATIONS, TESTIMONIES

As mentioned earlier, our message must *show* rather than *tell*. And a Texas evangelist certainly has made his message visible! In my book *Devotional Pursuits*, I wrote,

> Rev. Bill Lane who . . . preaches "hellfire, damnation, and brimstone" added something new to his "preachin'." Suddenly the not-so-hot minister became one of the hottest evangelists in the country. Literally. He set himself on fire while giving a sermon on hell. The idea caught on like wildfire and soon he was known to millions as the "Flaming Evangelist."
>
> Already, Rev. Lane has set himself on fire seventy-five times and has only been burnt badly once. He wears a specially treated undershirt and shirt to prevent the fire from burning through.
>
> While the flames are raging, Bill points to the crowd with a flaming finger and shouts, "You may not like what you are seeing, but imagine this for eternity!"

Rev. Lane claims five thousand people have come to Christ as a result of his burning message. I'm not about to recommend this as a persuasive evangelistic approach, but it does point out that people are changed when they are able to visualize the message.

When Christ became flesh and dwelt among us, He made abstract eternal truth, practical and earthy. We can't "see" God's balance of mercy and justice, but we can see Christ saving an adulterous woman from stoning. We can't see humanity's lack of purpose without God, but we can see lost sheep. We can't see a God who is dying to have a relationship with us, but we can see Christ crucified.

Christ's life not only revealed God, but His illustrations put flesh on heavenly truth. Rather than trying to explain faith, He pointed to mustard seeds and the mountains hugging the Sea of Galilee. Sin became visible as weeds and infectious yeast.

Rather than preaching a five-point sermon on hypocrisy, Christ spoke of whitewashed tombs filled with dead men's bones and everything unclean. Hypocrites were poisonous snakes. These word pictures communicate more truth than thousands of words. We can see whitewashed tombs. We can smell putrid flesh. We can hear the hiss of a cobra.

ILLUSTRATIONS THAT CHANGE LIVES
SHOW RATHER THAN TELL

"He was scared" tells us little. But "His stomach tightened and his pupils fixed on [whatever he's scared of]" does! "It was cold" tells us little. "His breath instantly froze into icicles on his mustache." Now that's cold! In Christ's stories we can hear the thunder and see the waves crashing into the wise man's house. We can see the foolish man's house collapse as waves eat away at its weak foundation.

Christ was a master of communication because He was able to take the abstract and turn it into something His listeners could see, hear, feel, taste, and touch. His illustrations breathed life into His words.

C. S. Lewis's Chronicles of Narnia brilliantly show the false promises of sin ("always winter but never Christmas"); the power of Christ in the lion Aslan, who "is not safe, but good"; and the atonement as the lion lays down his life for that little twit Edmund.

ILLUSTRATIONS THAT CHANGE LIVES TELL A GOOD STORY

Jesus' parable of the Good Samaritan is a wonderful example of a powerful story:

> A man was going down from Jerusalem to Jericho, when he fell into the hands of robbers. They stripped him of his clothes, beat him and went away, leaving him half dead. A priest happened to be going down the same road, and when he saw the man, he passed by on the other side. So too, a Levite, when he came to the place and saw him, passed by on the other side. But a Samaritan, as he traveled, came where the man was; and when he saw him, he took pity on him. He went to him and bandaged his wounds, pouring on oil and wine. Then he put the man on his own donkey, took him to an inn and took care of him. The next day he took out two silver coins and gave them to the innkeeper. "Look after him," he said, "and when I return, I will reimburse you for any extra expense you may have." (Luke 10:30–35)

Conflict

Without conflict, a story is like watching home video where nobody moves—they just sheepishly smile at the camera or try to hide behind Uncle Harold. Conflict takes many forms: man against man, man against God, man against society, man against ideology, man against ignorance, man against nature, or man against himself

Notice how Jesus' story of the Good Samaritan uses all of these conflicts. The man traveling from Jerusalem is attacked by robbers (man against man, man against God in disobeying the commandment not to steal) and is left half dead beneath the burning sun (man against nature). The Jews walk by the half-dead Samaritan because of their religious and racial prejudices (man against society, man against ignorance).

There may have been some struggles within the priest and Levite as to whether or not to assist this mugging victim (man against himself).

In each conflict, there is the *protagonist* (the person or thing the conflict comes up against) and an *antagonist* (the person or thing creating the conflict.) Only in two-dimensional fiction is the protagonist completely good and the antagonist completely evil. Abraham lied by saying his wife was his sister and then later slept with his wife's maid. David—the man after God's own heart—was an adulterer and murderer. Jeremiah suffered from deep depression.

The Cause of the Conflict

For a story to affect us, we must know what forces create the conflict. What drives the protagonist? The antagonist? For instance, let's take a look at the parable of the prodigal son:

There was a man who had two sons. The younger one said to his father, "Father, give me my share of the estate." So he divided his property between them.

Not long after that, the younger son got together all he had, set off for a distant country and there squandered his wealth in wild living. After he had spent everything, there was a severe famine in that whole country, and he began to be in need. So he went and hired himself out to a citizen of that country, who sent him to his fields to feed pigs. He longed to fill his stomach with the pods that the pigs were eating, but no one gave him anything.

When he came to his senses, he said, "How many of my father's hired men have food to spare, and here I am starving to death! I will set out and go back to my father and say to him: Father, I have sinned against heaven and against you. I am no longer worthy to be called your son; make me like one of your hired men." So he got up and went to his father.

But while he was still a long way off, his father saw him and was filled with compassion for him; he ran to his son, threw his arms around him and kissed him.

The son said to him, "Father, I have sinned against heaven and against you. I am no longer worthy to be called your son."

But the father said to his servants, "Quick! Bring the best robe and put it on him. Put a ring on his finger and sandals on his feet. Bring the fattened calf and kill it. Let's have a feast and celebrate. For this son of mine was dead and is alive again; he was lost and is found." So they began to celebrate.

Meanwhile, the older son was in the field. When he came near the house, he heard music and dancing. So he called one of the servants and asked him what was going on. "Your brother has come," he replied, "and your father has killed the fattened calf because he has him back safe and sound."

The older brother became angry and refused to go in. So his father went out and pleaded with him. But he answered his father, "Look! All these years I've been slaving for you and never disobeyed your orders. Yet you never gave me even a young goat so I could celebrate with my friends. But when this son of yours who has squandered your property with prostitutes comes home, you kill the fattened calf for him!"

"My son," the father said, "you are always with me, and everything I have is yours. But we had to celebrate and be glad, because this brother of yours was dead and is alive again; he was lost and is found." (Luke 15:11–31)

Notice that the prodigal son is driven by both good and evil forces— as all mortals are.

Good forces	Evil forces
His father's values	His independent spirit
Reality of what he had in his father's house	Allurement of the world
His conscience	Wild living

The careful balance between noble desires and the not-so-noble creates believable conflict. Peter was driven by a love for Christ and a fear of being associated with Him.

A writing book for Christians, written in the 1950s, declared, "Strong characters with strong purposes and fearless decisions make strong stories. Don't bother with any other kind." I'm afraid that would eliminate most of our favorite Bible stories.

ILLUSTRATIONS THAT CHANGE LIVES HAVE A CLEAR PLAN AND ORGANIZATION

Powerful stories are divided into three sections.

The Beginning

We are introduced to the characters, the setting, and the conflict. In the story of the Good Samaritan, we are given all three in just one concise sentence: "A man was going down from Jerusalem to Jericho, when he fell into the hands of robbers."

In a novel or short story, more would be told of the man: physical characteristics, age, family, politics, religion, lifestyle, finances, occupation, attitudes—everything that would explain his reaction to the conflict.

The beginning would also include "pointers" and "plants." Pointers are significant clues that seem insignificant at the time, but later in the story, the reader discovers, "Aha, now I see why. . . ." Notice that in the Good Samaritan, the significance of the man coming from Jerusalem is not apparent until a few verses later. Pointers make the development of the plot seem natural—not merely contrived.

"Plants" are physical objects or locations that are utilized as the story unfolds. As mentioned earlier, Moses' rod makes a wonderful plant throughout the book of Exodus. It is a common thread running through Moses' commissioning at the burning bush, the plagues, the escape through the Red Sea, and the finding of water in the desert.

The Middle

Here we find the conflict's complications and crisis. The beginning of the Good Samaritan leaves us with the man falling into the hands of robbers. We have a hint of the conflict to come. In the middle we have three scenes, each with its own conflict. We find man against man and man against nature as he is beaten and left half dead. Man against ideology, ignorance, and society arise as his hopes for rescue rise and fall. Finally, we see man against society. Will a Samaritan help a Jew?

Each scene includes conflict, which takes the protagonist to the final outcome.

The Ending

The author reveals the final decision or action in the conflict, and the effect of the outcome on the protagonist. Good illustrations don't have to be epic in length. The Good Samaritan is only five verses long. But it contains all the essential ingredients for a successful story.

The illustration always needs to make the message clear. "But didn't Christ purposely speak in vague illustrations on some occasions?" you might ask. True, but only because God intended to reveal the Messiah to the Jews first, then to the Gentiles. Once with His disciples, however, He explained each and every parable. Since all people groups are now to be evangelized and discipled, our illustrations must make the message clear. And Christ was very clear in many of His stories: "When the chief priests and the Pharisees heard Jesus' parables, they knew he was talking about them" (Matt. 21:45).

Some of the worst places to find illustrations are books of illustrations. Most are outdated, dry, or boring. Or, to show the problem rather than simply tell it, they are antique trunks filled with stale, suffocating dust. Fresh, humorous, up-to-date illustrations are abundant in magazines, newspapers, the Internet, song lyrics, personal experiences, and wherever people are being people.

Now we've researched our subject from all angles and perspectives, we've organized it, rewritten it so the prose flows, and have included illustrations that bring the message to life. But there are two more important ingredients for a persuasive book or sermon, as we'll see in the next two chapters.

PART 3
CHANGING
LIVES WITH
INTEGRITY

> *"Teacher," [the Pharisees] said, "we know you are a man of integrity and that you teach the way of God in accordance with the truth. You aren't swayed by men, because you pay no attention to who they are."*
>
> Matthew 22:16

10

DEMONSTRATING MORAL INTEGRITY AND PURE MOTIVES

A well-known pastor in our city was recently arrested and charged with child molesting. The paper emphasized there were *unproven* charges and that the pastor was *innocent* until proven guilty. However, emotional reaction was so intense that the trial was moved to another city with the media banned from the proceedings.

It's a tragedy no matter how the jury rules. Even if he is declared "not guilty," his integrity has been questioned in such a dramatic manner that it would seem impossible for him to return to that pastorate.

The apostle Paul was aware of the need for moral integrity and pure motives:

> You see, we are not like the many hucksters who preach for personal profit. We preach the word of God with sincerity and with Christ's authority, knowing that God is watching us. (2 Cor. 2:17 NLT)

> We put no stumbling block in anyone's path, so that our ministry will not be discredited. (2 Cor. 6:3)

> For we are taking pains to do what is right, not only in the

eyes of the Lord but also in the eyes of men. (2 Cor. 8:21)

Even though Christ was hated by the synagogue leaders, they were forced to admit He was a man of integrity (Matt. 22:16). How can we have such integrity? Our writing, and our *lives*, must convince our readers and listeners that we are spiritually and doctrinally sound.

SPIRITUALLY AND DOCTRINALLY SOUND

With more than 23,000 verses from which to choose, we can find a verse to prove just about any point on any subject. To prove the point, I asked my first youth group to read the book of Ecclesiastes and develop their own cult using out-of-context verses. The results were incredible!

One group had as its mission statement Ecclesiastes 10:19: "A feast is made for laughter, and wine makes life merry, but money is the answer for everything."

Another group's members were required to hold evangelistic services at the local animal shelter based on this verse: "For the fate of the sons of men and the fate of beasts is the same. As one dies so dies the other; indeed, they all have the same breath and there is no advantage for man over beast, for all is vanity" (Eccl. 3:19 NASB).

Hopefully the students learned these important lessons about Bible study:

Take the Common Meaning in the Original Languages

Words change over the years. Right now I would be terribly misunderstood if I said, "I'm feeling very gay today." Fifty years ago, it would have meant I was happy, joyous. In 2007 it means something *very* different. If I say, "That's a really bad car," I'm not saying it needs to be recalled for safety concerns. It's a really *cool* car (which doesn't refer to temperature at this time.) All these examples have the shelf life of milk!

It's the same with Scripture written thousands of years ago. For instance, let's take another verse often misinterpreted: "I do not permit a woman to teach or to have authority over a man; she must be silent" (1 Tim. 2:12). In AD 60 the word translated "authority" from the Greek actually had multiple meanings (and since this is the only time the word is used in the New Testament, it's impossible to determine how Paul used it from other contexts.)

Scott Baldwin, popular author on women's issues, noted several possible translations: to control, to dominate, to compel, to influence someone/thing, to domineer/play the tyrant, to grant authorization, to act independently, to assume authority over, to exercise one's own jurisdiction, to flout the authority of, to commit murder. He concluded the most likely translation is "to have authority over" or "to domineer."

Catherine Kroeger, a Greek scholar and founder of Christians for Biblical Equality, argued that *authenteÿ* is an erotic term best translated "to engage in fertility practices." She later changed her interpretation to mean "proclaim oneself author of a man" in response to "a Gnostic notion of Eve as creator of Adam" (see 2 Tim. 2:13). Dr. Kroeger also noted that the word, used at the time in court briefs, refers to "self murder" or suicide. L. E. Wilshire studied 314 references to *authenteÿ* and concluded it originally was connected with murder and suicide, but later to the "broader concept of criminal behavior."

Thus, those supportive of women in ministry interpret it to mean "dominate," which Paul strictly forbade, since men and women are to be viewed as equals (Gal. 3:28) and "submit to one another" (Eph. 5:21). Fundamentalists interpret the word to denote a hierarchy; women must not be in a supervisory role over men. (However, the word didn't mean hierarchy until AD 300.)

The best we can conclude is that there is no precise definition for the word.

You don't have to be a Hebrew, Aramaic, or Greek expert to study the meanings of words at the time of biblical writing. (I passed Greek "magna cum grace.") There are many excellent online lexicons.

Take the Cultural Context of the Passage

Let's continue with 1 Timothy 2:12. In that culture, women were not allowed a formal education, so virtually all women in Ephesus at that time were illiterate. This, of course, made being a woman teacher a bit difficult!

Melanie Kierstead, of Asbury College, also argued that Paul wrote the controversial passage to address the matriarchal culture of Asia Minor, and particularly Ephesus, where the gods were all women and the human men were ceremonially castrated. Thus, these are specific instructions for a specific people (those in the Ephesus church) at a specific time (first century) in a particular place (Asia Minor, where the temple of Dianna, goddess worship, and matriarchal dominance were). Other scholars, however, believe temple prostitution was no longer practiced in AD 60 Ephesus.

Good commentaries will provide the cultural context of passages. With Paul's letters, we are listening in on one side of a conversation and need to know what was happening on the other end of the conversation to provide context. As kids, listening to one side of my mother's phone conversations, my brother and I concluded Mom was a CIA operative with her blind, Middle Eastern chiropractor her contact.

Take the Broadest, Most Documented Position

If you have a church filled with illiterate women who are recent converts from goddess worship (or ex-temple prostitutes), 1 Timothy 1:12 is wise advice for *that* church at *that* time.

But if you look at the entire Bible's view of women, you see many leaders and teachers: prophets (Miriam, Deborah, Huldah, Isaiah's wife, Philip's four daughters), a military leader and judge (Deborah), disciples (Mary, Martha, Joanna, Mary Magdalene, Susanna, and "many more"), a deacon (Priscilla), and a church leader (Lydia). Then you have to deal with

Acts 2:17–18, which is a fulfillment of Joel's prophecy: "Your sons and *daughters* will prophesy."

Following these three principles will clear up many apparent contradictions. Ecclesiastes is a journal of a man on a spiritual journey to find meaning (and later finds money "vanity"). So, his writing that "money is the answer to everything" is not contrary to Jesus' teaching that we can't serve God and money or Paul's observation that "the love of money is the root of all evil."

Each time I start a new book, I buy a cheap paperback edition of the New Testament and use a highlighter to mark every passage that addresses my subject. That way, I am getting an overview of the entire Testament and not verses ripped out of context. (One of my professors argued that concordances are the greatest source of heresy, since they allow people to find verses that support their case without looking at the broader context of the entire Bible.)

A CREDIBLE MESSAGE NEEDS A CREDIBLE MESSENGER

To truly have credibility with an audience, our writing or speaking must be well-informed, logical, and tasteful. And we must live ethical, moral lives marked with humility, compassion for others, and pure motives.

Well-informed

I had a difficult time listening to a famous speaker after he announced the "hypothalamus is located at the base of your nose." Not *my* nose—or anyone else's either. It's located in the middle of the brain (and regulates metabolism and body temperature, as well as hunger and thirst). The speaker had undercut his credibility with his inaccurate information, which brought the rest of his talk into question.

Unfortunately, many Christians have lost credibility by passing on urban legends as truth:

"Madalyn Murray O'Hair is petitioning to have all religious broadcasting taken off the airwaves" (she was apparently murdered in 1995!).

"The Procter and Gamble logo is a satanic symbol."

"Siberian oil well drillers have lowered a microphone down a two-mile shaft and recorded hell's wailing and gnashing of teeth."

"NASA scientists discovered the lost day from Joshua 10."

"President George W. Bush took a half hour off from glad-handing supporters at a 'thank you' dinner to witness for Christ to a teenage boy."

No wonder Christians have little credibility! To quote the first rule of journalism, "If your mother says she loves you, check it out." (And with cloning, in vitro fertilization, and genetic engineering, make sure she's your mother.)

John Wesley emphasized the need to be well informed. He required his pastors to spend at least five hours a day in reading material *other* than the Bible. To those who objected by saying, "I read only the Bible," Wesley had this answer:

Then you ought to teach others to read only the Bible and by parity of reason, to hear only the Bible. But if so, you need preach no more. And if you need no book but the Bible, you are above St. Paul. He wanted other [books] too. "Bring the books," he says, "but especially the parchments."

Remember that Christ's disciples were not "unschooled men" as charged by the Sanhedrin. Unschooled?! They had just completed a three-year, twenty-four-hours-a-day cram course from God's own Son. (And we thought college was tough!)

Neither was Stephen, the first Christian martyr, unschooled. The members of the synagogue (the brain trust of Judaism) "could not stand up against his wisdom or the Spirit by whom he spoke" (Acts 6:10). He had learned his lessons well from the daily teaching of the apostles. And Paul had not only been educated by Gamaliel, the leader of the Sanhedrin, but with another of Christ's three-year crash courses, this time in the desert of Arabia.

Education is essential in effectively communicating! A student may be "called" by God to be a missionary doctor, but I'm not letting her take out my appendix until she has finished her residency. The same is true for those who wield the pen, which is mightier than the sword, and the Bible—a double-edged sword—which is exponentially mightier than both pens and swords.

Good Logic

Chapters 5 and 6 are devoted to this important tool.

Good Taste

A convention speaker provided glaring proof that good taste is essential in writing to change lives. He was stressing that we need to listen to *what* people are saying rather than *how* they say it. The three hundred ministers were absorbing every word.

But then he illustrated his point with a military man's comment on one of his sermons: "That was the best [bleep] [bleep] [bleeping] sermon I've ever heard." Unfortunately, he didn't "bleep" out the vulgar words. Immediately, the convention speaker lost his audience. Although he had other valuable points to make, his poor taste eclipsed everything he said.

Be aware of your audience's sensitivities. What can be written in the *Wittenburg Door,* Christianity's version of *Mad* magazine, will probably not work in the *Herald of Holiness.*

Ethical, Moral, Godly Lives

Paul provided a helpful checklist for those who wish to effectively communicate the gospel. They should be

❏ Above reproach   ❏ Not lovers of money
❏ Temperate   ❏ Good managers of their families
❏ Self-controlled   ❏ Parents of obedient children
❏ Respectable   ❏ Not recent converts
❏ Hospitable   ❏ Examples in speech
❏ Able to teach   ❏ Examples in life
❏ Not given to much wine   ❏ Examples in faith
❏ Not violent but gentle   ❏ Examples in purity
❏ Not quarrelsome   ❏ Serious

Humility

Paul encouraged us to live and write with humility:

Do nothing out of selfish ambition or vain conceit, but in humility consider others better than yourselves. Each of you should look not only to your own interests, but also to the interests of others.

Your attitude should be the same as that of Christ Jesus:

Who, being in very nature God, did not consider equality with God something to be grasped, but made himself nothing, taking the very nature of a servant. (Phil. 2:3–7)

I love the term used to describe the Holy Spirit: *paraclete*. It is one who comes alongside. As writers and speakers, that is a powerful posture to take. We "come alongside" our readers or listeners. Not ahead of them. Not above them. But beside them.

Compassion for the Audience

Paul admonished us to "speak the truth in love." I'm afraid the so-called liberals do a good job of loving but not always so good speaking the truth. So-called conservatives are much better at speaking the truth than doing it in love.

The preacher from Topeka, Kansas, who shows up at military funerals with his "God Hates America" and "God Hates [slur for homosexuals]" is an extreme example of ignoring this admonition. He's also picketed in New York City several times since September 11, 2001, with signs that read "Thank God For Sept. 11." Then there's the TV evangelist and self-professed spokesperson for evangelicals who called the singer Madonna a "despicable prostitute" and gay comedian Ellen DeGeneres, "Ellen DeGenerate." And another TV evangelist and also self-professed spokesperson for evangelicals called for the assassination of Venezuela dictator Hugo Chavez.

First, if homosexuals, rock stars, and dictators are—for the sake of argument—our theological, political, and/or ideological enemies, how did Christ teach us to respond? "But love your enemies, do good to them. . . . Then your reward will be great, and you will be sons of the Most High, because he is kind to the ungrateful and wicked. Be merciful, just as your Father is merciful. Do not judge, and you will not be judged. Do not condemn, and you will not be condemned" (Luke 6:35–37).

Second, what did Paul say our attitude should be toward those outside the faith? "Be wise in the way you act toward outsiders; make the most of every opportunity. Let your conversation be always full of grace, seasoned with salt, so that you may know how to answer everyone" (Col. 4:5–6).

Peter added, "And if someone asks about your Christian hope, always be ready to explain it. But do this in a gentle and respectful way" (1 Peter 3:15–16 NLT).

If we are going to change lives, our approach must be with love, grace, and gentleness. And, as my homiletics professor used to warn, "If you're going to preach that sinners are going to hell, do it with a tear in your eye."

David Augsburger, in *Caring Enough to Confront*, poetically agrees:

> I differ with you
> > (to differ is not to reject)
> I disagree with you
> > (to disagree is not to attack)
> I will confront you
> > (to confront is to compliment)
> I will invite change
> > (to change is to grow)

Augsburger made it clear that if we care, we *must* confront. And so does Scripture: "Dear brothers and sisters, if another believer is overcome by some sin, you who are godly should gently and humbly help that person back onto the right path" (Gal. 6:1 NLT).

Pure Motives

How we confront and the *motive* for that confrontation are as important as the message itself. That's why the apostle Paul wrote,

> Some are preaching out of jealousy and rivalry. But others preach about Christ with pure motives. They preach because they love me, for they know I have been appointed to defend the Good News. Those others do not have pure motives as they preach about Christ. They preach with selfish ambition, not sincerely, intending to make my chains more painful to me. But that doesn't matter. Whether their motives are false or genuine, the message about Christ is being preached either way, so I rejoice. And I will continue to rejoice. (Phil. 1:15–18 NLT)

> For we speak as messengers approved by God to be entrusted with the Good News. Our purpose is to please God, not people.

He alone examines the motives of our hearts. Never once did we try to win you with flattery, as you well know. (1 Thess. 2:4–5 NLT)

And the Lord's servant must not quarrel; instead, he must be kind to everyone, able to teach, not resentful. Those who oppose him he must gently instruct, in the hope that God will grant them repentance leading them to a knowledge of the truth, and that they will come to their senses and escape from the trap of the devil, who has taken them captive to do his will. (2 Tim. 2:24–26)

Samuel Johnson graphically pointed out that the only genuine motive for the Christian must be to please God:

If I fling half a crown to a beggar with the intention to break his head, and he picks it up and buys [food] with it, the physical effect is good, but, with respect to me, the action is very wrong. So, religious exercises, if not performed with an intention to please God, avail us nothing."

So, in conclusion, from the King James Watkins Version,

Though I write with the eloquence of men and of angels, but have not love, I am become as a clattering printer or a clanging press. And though I have the gift of all knowledge and understand the books of Daniel and Revelation, and if my words can move mountains, but have not love, I am nothing. And though I give my royalties to relief organizations and struggling writers, and am invited to speak at national conventions, but have not love, if profits me nothing.

Love indeed must be the motivation for everything we say and write, as we'll discover in the next chapter.

*For the appeal we make does not spring
from error or impure motives, nor are
we trying to trick you.*

1 Thessalonians 2:3

11

DEMONSTRATING PURE MOTIVATION VS. MANIPULATION

I'm a hopeless idealist! (It's probably the result of growing up in the 60s when we had every intention of ending all wars and living in love and peace. Groovy!) So, I'd like to think that God's love should be the only motivating factor to move people to righteous actions.

I'm also a pragmatist and realize that many are not spiritually mature enough to do something without mixed motives. Even the apostle Paul wasn't completely sure of his own motivations:

> I care very little if I am judged by you or by any human court; indeed, I do not even judge myself. My conscience is clear, but that does not make me innocent. It is the Lord who judges me. Therefore judge nothing before the appointed time; wait till the Lord comes. He will bring to light what is hidden in darkness and will expose the motives of men's hearts. At that time each will receive his praise from God. (1 Cor. 4:3–5)

So, do the spiritually immature need to be motivated at their level of development? Is this why Paul used pride and peer pressure to motivate the Corinthian church to give (2 Cor. 8)? And Philemon is filled with motivation by guilt! Is that any different from some TV evangelists who preach "seed faith" giving to their so-called ministries? Does the end justify the means? And what exactly are the ends? Edward Bernays, a nephew of Sigmund Freud, is considered the father of public relations. His ends and means are rather frightening. He told *World* magazine:

> The conscious and intelligent manipulation of the organized habits and opinions of the masses is an important element in democratic society. Those who manipulate the unseen mechanism of society constitute an invisible government which is the true ruling power of the country. [I am] one of the small number of persons . . . who understand the mental processes and social patterns of the masses. [I] pull the wires which control the public mind.

The leader of a Christian fund-raising group isn't far from Bernays' belief that the end justifies any means: "We know that people will give more to this ministry out of greed than a pure heart. Since we're using their money for godly purposes, we don't mind appealing to greed to get it."

Secular writer Vance Packard would question that approach.

> What is the morality of playing upon the hidden weaknesses and frailties—such as our anxieties, aggressive feelings, dread of nonconformity, and infantile hangovers? Specifically, what are the ethics of businesses that shape campaigns designed to thrive on these weaknesses they have diagnosed? (*The Hidden Persuaders*)

Martin Carlton, in *Why People Give,* addressed Packard's questions and confronted greedy TV evangelists:

> "You can't raise money for high purposes with low motives." This is not so. You can, but should you? What happens to the

giver as a person before God when he does the right thing for the wrong motive? Does the use of any kind of motivation not consistent with Christian ideals tend to foster a spirit of "work-righteousness" on the part of the giver—as though he was earning his way with God?

A BLURRY LINE

So what is the line between motivation and manipulation? Unfortunately, it is not always distinct. In fact, it is often no line at all, but a blur of subtle shades of gray blending into the black and white. Paul, however, gave some practical advice in making the distinction:

> When I first came to you, dear brothers and sisters, I didn't use lofty words and impressive wisdom to tell you God's secret plan. . . . my message and my preaching were very plain. Rather than using clever and persuasive speeches, I relied only on the power of the Holy Spirit. I did this so you would trust not in human wisdom but in the power of God. (1 Cor. 2:1, 4–5 NLT)

If proclaiming the good news was simply a matter of marketing, then we should assign the "gospel account" to the best New York ad agency. But there is more involved here than marketing research, the right media mix, ten million dollars in cash prizes, and a talking duck.

Thus the paradox. Human manipulation works! We can change behavior by tapping into those "felt needs" cataloged in chapter 2. But the effect of human effort is often short-lived without the power of the Holy Spirit working in the life of the sender and receiver. With this in mind, Paul made a strong statement against manipulation:

> Rather, we have renounced secret and shameful ways; we do not use deception, nor do we distort the word of God. On the contrary,

by setting forth the truth plainly we commend ourselves to every man's conscience in the sight of God. And even if our gospel is veiled, it is veiled to those who are perishing. (2 Cor. 4:2–3)

AN ETHICAL APPROACH TO CHANGING LIVES

To be ethical in our attempts to change lives, I believe we must set for the truth plainly, appeal to everyone's conscience, and respect everyone's right to reject the truth.

Set Forth the Truth Plainly

For instance, the vacuum cleaner salesman did not "set forth the truth plainly." First, this unethical character called my wife asking if we would like the parsonage carpet cleaned—free! Lois thoroughly interrogated him as to the catch. "No catch—it's merely a company promotion." Great! A carpet-cleaning company wants some free publicity.

I was right in the middle of finishing Sunday's message when Lois called to say there was an irate vacuum cleaner salesman at the door. "Vacuum cleaner salesman?!"

"He's the guy who's going to clean our carpets. He says you have to be here for the demonstration before he cleans our carpets."

"Vacuum cleaner salesman?! 'Rugs-R-Us' never said they were selling vacuum cleaners!" And so, for the next two hours we endured a high-pressure sales pitch. He showed us pictures of microscopic creatures that threatened our very lives unless they were beaten senseless and vacuumed up by the Rugs-R-Us Super Sucker 7000. But wait, there's more. It would purify the air, sanitize our bathroom, humidify the house, paint our car—everything to make this a safer, cleaner world to live in.

We finally persuaded him we weren't buying and merely wanted our carpets cleaned. He grudgingly cleaned our carpets and stormed out, muttering something about beating senseless and sucking up customers.

Rugs-R-Us didn't make a sale because we resented their deceptive approach. Unfortunately, some of our evangelistic approaches are not much different. Some manipulate non-Christian friends into attending concerts, films, and seminars without mentioning it is a *Christian* concert, film, or seminar. Some befriend neighbors with "*soul*-winning" as the *sole* motivation. Some groups offer retreats that are little more than propaganda sessions.

Paul warned us to avoid secret, shameful, and deceptive methods.

Appeal to Everyone's Conscience

Those writers and speakers who use manipulation often rely on massive doses of guilt. At this point we need to ask if the guilt is man-made or God-given. Paul made the distinction in 2 Corinthians 7:9–10: "Your sorrow led you to repentance. For you became sorrowful as God intended and so were not harmed in any way by us. Godly sorrow brings repentance that leads to salvation and leaves no regret, but worldly sorrow brings death."

Psychologists claim our upbringing produces two accusers: the "ideal self" (our ideas and our parents' expectations of what we should be) and the "punitive self" (the "little parent" still within us shaking its finger when we don't measure up to our ideal self). Any time we violate the ideal self, the punitive self begins to tell us we're no good, people will be disappointed with us, we are "wretches" and "worms," and that God won't love us if we act like that.

But God never makes a Christian feel guilty. It is Satan who is our accuser (Rev. 12:10) and God who is our advocate (1 John 2:1). Paul wrote, "Who will bring any charge against those whom God has chosen? It is God who justifies" (Rom. 8:33).

As mentioned above, Paul also wrote that "worldly sorrow" leads to death, but "godly sorrow" leads to loving conformity to God's will. Bruce Narramore and Bill Count, in *Freedom from Guilt,* made these important distinctions:

	Psychological guilt	Constructive sorrow
Person in primary focus	Self	God and others
Attitudes or actions in primary focus	Past misdeeds	Damage done to other or our future correct deeds
Motivation for change (if any)	To avoid feeling bad (guilt feelings)	To help others, to promote our growth, or to do God's will (love feelings)
Attitude toward self	Anger and frustration	Love and respect combined with concern
Result	(a) External change (b) Stagnation due to paralyzing effect of guilt (c) Further rebellion	Repentance and change based on an attitude of love, mutual respect

I need to be careful that I'm not using guilt to manipulate, but allowing God to lovingly motivate my readers through my message.

Respect Everyone's Right to Reject Truth

Salesmen are trained to keep you from resisting their pitch. They will never ask, "Do you want to buy the Rugs-R-Us Super Sucker 7000?" The questions go something like, "Are you concerned about your family's health? You would like to rid your home of microscopic creatures, wouldn't you? Would you like it in black, gray, or mauve? Will that be check or credit card? Would you like it delivered Monday or Tuesday?" And the coup de grâce, "Today only, we're offering $100 off the Rugs-R-Us Super Sucker 7000. You would like to save $100, wouldn't you? Tomorrow it will be full price."

I'm offended by those questions. (What fool is going to answer, "I kinda like having my home filled with microscopic creatures. They're low-maintenance pets."). And I am put off by the pressure. Yet it sounds a lot like "You do want to live eternally, don't you? Do you have any assurance that you won't die tonight? You could walk out that door and be hit by a Mac truck."

Em Griffin, in *Getting Together*, warned,

> Just behavior means not imposing our beliefs or standards
> upon all our followers. The key word is imposing. We may try
> to influence; in fact we should. But these attempts at persua-
> sion must always leave inviolate another's free right to choose.

Bill Hybels, of Willow Creek Community Church, agrees. He
suggests opening the valve of living water a little at a time, rather than
swamping the listener with a flash flood.

> [Then] let him think it over, see the implications, ask ques-
> tions, talk with others about it. If you force him to make a
> decision in forty minutes, he may say no, not on the basis of
> the gospel, but on the basis that he didn't have enough time to
> give it adequate thought.

We see Jesus doing this with the rich young man who asked, "Teacher,
what good thing must I do to get eternal life?"

> Jesus replied, "If you want to be perfect, go, sell your posses-
> sions and give to the poor, and you will have treasure in
> heaven. Then come, follow me."
>
> When the young man heard this, he went away sad,
> because he had great wealth.
>
> Then Jesus said to his disciples, "I tell you the truth, it is hard
> for a rich man to enter the kingdom of heaven." (Matt. 19:21–23)

Notice that Jesus didn't argue with him. He didn't say, "Wait! Maybe
that's a bit extreme. How 'bout this? If you'll tithe you can have eternal
life." No. He let him walk away.

In John 3, we find Nicodemus coming to Jesus to ask what he

must do to receive eternal life. As mentioned in chapter 7, there's no record in the chapter that Nicodemus became a believer during that encounter. We do, however, read the following in John 19:38–40:

> Later, Joseph of Arimathca asked Pilate for the body of Jesus. Now Joseph was a disciple of Jesus, but secretly because he feared the Jews. With Pilate's permission, he came and took the body away. He was accompanied by Nicodemus, the man who earlier had visited Jesus at night. Nicodemus brought a mixture of myrrh and aloes, about seventy-five pounds. Taking Jesus' body, the two of them wrapped it, with the spices, in strips of linen.

At some point in the transpiring sixteen chapters, Nicodemus became a follower. But not necessarily during chapter 3.

Finally, Fred Smith observed the distinction between manipulation and motivation:

> The difference is you can substitute the word "thirst" for motivation but not manipulation. Unless you're satisfying someone's thirst, you are probably manipulating rather than motivating. I can motivate with integrity when I am bringing to consciousness a genuine thirst. (*The Manipulation Game*)

Let's make sure we're motivating, not manipulating.

PART 4
CHANGING LIVES
THROUGH . . .

Do you have the gift of speaking?
Then speak as though God himself
were speaking through you.

1 Peter 4:11 NLT

12
CHANGING LIVES
THROUGH . . .
SPEAKING

Pop quiz! Take out a clean sheet of paper and a Number 2 pencil and answer the following:

1. What do you remember from your high school commencement speech?

2. What did the president say at the last press conference?

3. What was the main point of your pastor's sermon last Sunday? (Extra points if you can remember all ten points.)

So, how did you do? If you failed the quiz, it was actually the *speaker* who failed the quiz. Did he or she apply the principles we've discussed so far: knowing the goal, knowing the audience, and knowing the techniques of effective communication?

All the principles of this book apply to verbal as well as printed communication. There are, however, some unique elements of verbal communication that makes it the most effective mode of persuasion.

CONNECTION

Work the Room

First, an example of disconnection. I have been a fan of a certain author for several years. His book is marked up, highlighted, dog-eared, and generally falling apart from my reading it at least ten times. I had the chance to hear him at the Christian Booksellers Association convention. He's as brilliant on the stage as on the page.

But immediately following his talk, he was hustled off the stage by his handlers. It took showing my press credentials to three different people to finally get to meet him backstage. When I asked him to autograph my beat-up book, he glared at it and told me to get a copy of the revised edition. I never asked him my intended question — would he be available to speak at a writers conference I direct.

What makes speaking so effective is the connection, getting to see and hear the person in, well, person. But there's a danger of the speaker's simply being a performer rather than a person. That's why the least effective speakers are those who fly in, fly off, and fly out. There's no real connection.

So, whether you're a conference speaker or a Sunday school teacher, it's important to interact with your "audience" outside of the speech or teaching time. While Jesus occasionally spoke to crowds of five thousand men, not counting women and children, He spent a good deal of time with His inner circle of three — Peter, James, and John. They were privy to His glorious transformation as well as His agony in the Garden of Gethsemane. Then there was the circle of twelve apostles as well as 120 men and women He counted as disciples. Finally, the large crowds. Jesus knew the most effective persuasion occurs one-to-one or in small groups.

Our effectiveness dramatically increases if we spend some time with our audience before taking the stage or the lectern.

I was convinced of this while teaching in children's church. Nick was a totally disruptive seven-year-old with no church background. I decided to visit him in his home. He proudly showed me a beat-up guitar with four of the six strings missing. "I've got a guitar just like yours, Pastor Jim." He beamed. I offered to get some new strings for him and clean it up. When I brought it to children's church the next Sunday, this formerly disruptive child looked at his guitar newly strung and polished with awe and announced, "Pastor Jim, if any kids mouth off to you or act up, I'll beat the [bleep] out of them for you." Not exactly the response I was looking for, but Nick was a model children's church member after that.

Another time, while I was teaching a writing seminar in India, a radical Hindu kept interrupting asking the host why he had brought "these Americans" to teach Indians to write. My friend Cec Murphey and I sat with him at lunch and tried to take an interest in his life and ask how we could help him become a better writer. By the end of the week, he wanted his picture taken with his "American friends."

So, before a talk, I try to introduce myself to conferees and ask, "So, what would you like to learn today? How can I help you?"

And, it's just as important to be available after the lesson or lecture.

Maintain Eye Contact

If you're uncomfortable making eye contact with your audience, try looking over the tops of their heads so at least you seem to be looking in their direction. The pros learn to lock eyes with individuals for a sentence or two at a time, then move on to another person—rather than looking like a lighthouse beacon, constantly in motion.

CONFIDENCE

While I was riding with some "big name" authors on the way from the airport to the conference center, we began talking about our greatest fears. Number one—for everyone in the van—was being exposed as a complete fraud. One well-known author explained, "We come to these conferences and people view us as these confident and competent writers, when deep inside, we're totally insecure and intimidated by our so-called fans." Another best-selling author (you'd know his name if I told you) added, "Yeah, when I get on the stage, I become a 'best-selling author' and 'popular speaker.' They expect me to be a certain way, and so I become who they want. Then I go back to my room and return to being that insecure and intimidated person."

Perhaps that's unique to writers, who tend to feel more comfortable in front of a computer screen than a conference hall, but I suspect it applies to many public speakers. But students want a speaker who is confident and comfortable. So play the role of confident public speaker: Never ever apologize for nervousness, inadequacy, or anything else. The audience wants you to succeed. After all, they've come to hear this competent speaker or preacher.

Jerry Seinfeld noted that people fear speaking in public more than death. So, therefore, they would rather be in the coffin than delivering the eulogy. I suspect that most of the fear comes from two sources. The first is a lack of preparation, and second is a lack of experience. For the first few years of speaking, I became physically ill before going on.

One thing that helped was assuming a relaxed posture. When a TV director would start counting down on his fingers, "Five seconds to air, four, three, two . . ." I would intentionally throw one leg over my knee, lean back, and try to appear as relaxed as possible for the interview. And, my weak mind would be fooled into thinking I was cool, calm, and collected. In the same way, if I have the sides of the lectern in a death grip, my mind thinks *stress*.

Consider taking a class on public speaking or joining a local Toastmasters group to give you confidence and experience. And Liz Curtis Higgs, a brilliant and hilarious speaker, has a very practical chapter on speaking in the book I edited, *Writers on Writing*.

CONTENT

Twenty or more years ago, a good speech or sermon contained three points. That shifted in later years to one point. Now Leonard Sweet suggests that a memorable message has one picture. We live in a visual society, so persuasive talk must be seen as well as heard.

For instance, people remember only 10 percent of what they hear, 30 percent of what they see, 50 percent of what they see and hear, and 70 percent of they see, hear, and say. That's why it's important to be more than a talking head.

Use Illustrations

Just as in writing, real-life illustrations put flesh on the facts and add emotion to information. (See chapter 9.)

Use Props

First and foremost, you're the prop, the visual. Move around the platform rather than remaining rigidly behind the lectern. Movement keeps an audience's attention. (Use restraint, though. You're not Mick Jagger of the Rolling Stones, prowling the platform, either!)

Use PowerPoint, use objects. For my message on overcoming the "giants" in publishing, I pass around a leather shepherd's bag with smooth stones to make my points. All walk away with a smooth stone that hopefully reminds them that they are giant killers.

Get the Audience Talking

During that same talk, at the conclusion of each point, I encourage them to shout, "I'm a giant killer!" They're now hearing, seeing, and saying, which boosts retention from 20 percent to 70 percent. Elicit responses from your audience.

Distribute Handouts

Handouts are the most effective—other than a recording of the presentation—to increase retention.

CONVERSATION

I mentioned earlier about putting on an act of being comfortable in front of the Sunday school class or stadium event. But it can't come across as a performance!

Speaking Is about Communication, Not Performance

I used to pray, "Father, help me do well." In other words, "Make me look good!" That's probably the third cause of stage fright in public speaking. We want to give a perfectly polished performance, so the pressure is on!

Now I find myself praying, "Father, help me be helpful." I may totally bomb as far as delivery, but if lives are changed—and that's what this book is all about—then I have more than succeeded. And that takes the pressure off.

Speaking Is a Conversation, Not a Soliloquy

The shouting, fire-breathing preachers of the past are just that—the past. People today do not want to be preached at. That's why one homiletics professor suggests using your "indoor voice."

And it's not, again, a performance. Most professional speakers have been delivering the same talks for years, so they have the material down cold so they can speak without notes. But local pastors who present a new message every Sunday will probably have to make more use of notes. The safest way, of course, is to speak from a manuscript, but that can come across as dull and lifeless. (On sensitive subjects, however, you may want to read portions so anyone asking, "What did that speaker say?!" can know exactly what the speaker said.) Or hide your notes in your Bible or jot your main points on the margins of your Bible. For a few years at a local church, I used white boards sitting on the front pew as cue cards. (And since nobody ever sits on the front pew, no one knew.)

Even though your material is well planned and rehearsed, it must come across as casual conversation.

I would, however, recommend that you write out or memorize the first and last paragraphs of your talk. Planes crash on takeoff and landing—and so do talks. We've all been in churches or conferences where the speaker keeps doing "touch and go" landings. He says, "in conclusion," but then pulls up abruptly as he approaches the runway and seems in a perpetual holding pattern not able to bring his talk in for a safe landing. By writing out or memorizing the first and last paragraphs of your talk, you can have a smooth takeoff and a safe landing.

Speaking Is Two-way Communication

Speaking creates energy not present in the written word. Reading a book or an article is a solitary experience. But when you are surrounded by hundreds of other people reacting to the message, there is an energy and excitement. If only one or two laugh at your joke in a class of ten, there's not much of a response. But if you're in a crowd of a few hundred and 10 to 20 percent laugh, it becomes contagious. That's why I fear speaking to small crowds and love speaking to several hundred.

And because you're receiving feedback from "yeahs" to yawns, you can quickly adapt your presentation by picking up or slowing down the tempo, explaining a point that's eliciting looks of confusion, or skipping minor points to quickly conclude. (If you haven't struck oil in twenty minutes, stop boring!)

It's also important to allow time for questions and answers. Again, with writing, there's no opportunity for the reader to say, "I didn't quite understand by what you meant by . . .". But in speaking, there's the chance to clarify any confusion or address collateral issues.

CONVICTION

Finally, spoken communication has the advantage of tone of voice and body language that communicates your conviction, the *pathos*. A reader won't hear the emotion in your voice or see the tear in your eye.

So, in-person communication (even if it's through video conferencing) is the most effective mode of persuasion, but as we'll discuss in the next chapter, it is not the most efficient. Both are important.

*And he departed, and began to publish in
Decapolis how great things Jesus had
done for him: and all men did marvel.*
Mark 5:20 KJV

13
CHANGING LIVES
THROUGH . . .
WRITING

Speaking may be the most effective mode of persuasion, but it's not the most efficient.

For instance, I recently spoke to one hundred people at a seminar. I spent a day working on the talk and then one day at the nearby district campground delivering it. So, my ratio of impact was fifty people per day.

That same week, I spent a day writing an article for *Decision* magazine, which reaches 1.8 million readers. To reach that many at one hundred people at a time, I would have to speak 18,000 days in a row or for 4,931 years! My ratio of impact was exponentially greater.

And there is the advantage that the talk is somewhat permanent when put into print. Online writing is even better since it's available indefinitely, long after the magazine is in the recycle bin, to a worldwide audience.

So, writing is more efficient, but it's also more difficult. Your toolbox is virtually empty! There's no body language, which constitutes over 50 percent of our daily communication. There's no tone of voice, which communicates about 30 percent of our meaning. And, there's no video or audio, so reading is like watching TV with no sound or picture. Only 10 percent of communication's impact is the actual words. So, we have one tool—black splotches on white paper or pixels on a computer screen. Maybe that's why authors have written

> Writing is the hardest way of earning a living, with the possible exception of wrestling alligators. (Olin Miller)

> There ain't nothing more to write about, and I am rotten glad of it, because if I'd a knowed what a trouble it was to make a book, I wouldn't a tackled it, and ain't a going to no more. (Huckleberry Finn in *The Adventures of Huckleberry Finn*)

And publication is even harder. Only 1 percent of wannabe writers are published. Of that number, 1 percent actually make a living at it. (Part of the reason for these discouraging statistics is that there are fewer publishers, publishing fewer titles, by fewer authors. But mostly, it's because there are simply so many terrible writers submitting so many terrible manuscripts.)

But writing persuasively is not impossible—it's just hard work with very few tools.

WORD PICTURES

A persuasive writer must create the video and audio for the reader through powerful word pictures, anecdotes, and dialogue. And, some would argue, reading is actually far more effective (and enjoyable) than mindlessly watching TV, since one's imagination is far superior to the flat-screen depiction of the story.

Here are two of my attempts to vividly visualize a message. The first was written after one of the first TV evangelist scandals in 1988 and picked up by several publications after the most recent.

PEDESTALS

Thousands
cheer,
chant,
and clap
as one of their own
is proudly carried toward the
lofty pedestal.
The audience
urges him
up the stairway,
step by step,
higher and higher,
far above the masses
on the prominent platform.
The media is there
with lights,
cameras
and prime-time coverage.
Publishers huddle
around the base,
for they know
pedestal-people
sell well.
The crowds
on satellite hookups
hang on
every last word,
for he seems
so close to eternity.
Yet he feels

unsure,

unworthy,

afraid

and very alone . . .

But at that height

no one notices,

no one questions,

no one confronts.

And so,

in a split second,

the trap door swings,

the noose tightens,

the crowd gasps.

Undeterred, the mob moves on

to build more pedestals;

to encourage another

of their own

up the starlit steps.

But mostly

to wonder

why those

at the pinnacle

keep falling

from the heights.

The image of pedestals becoming gallows is shocking and, hope-fully, a powerful and cautionary picture. It certainly cured me of ever wanting to be a famous "pedestal" person!

In this second example, I tried to take something very cerebral and philosophical—the argument between "pro-choice" and "pro-life" proponents—and make it visible with word pictures. (And I also tried to use the principle from chapter 8 about using humorous incongruity to make a point.)

PLANNED BANK ROBBERY

We hear a lot about "pro-choice" on the evening news and in sound bites from politicians. We, too, want to avoid "legislating values and claiming there are moral absolutes."

Ethics is a personal choice, not a political or religious concern. That's why we've established "Planned Bank Robbery." Now, we personally don't approve of bank robbery, but we don't want to inflict our morals on anyone else either.

It must be a personal decision of each individual.

Education is the key, since our studies reveal that 99 percent of senior high teens know that banks are robbed. But it is shocking the number of teens who don't know *how* banks are robbed. Or even how to load a .357 Magnum, drive a getaway car, or demand, "Give me all of your unmarked, non-sequentially-ordered twenty-dollar bills." Young people need to know the wide range of career options available to them.

And we're also concerned that a lot of young people are robbing banks without proper protection. Personal injury and irresponsibility are much greater crimes than actually knocking over the First National. At Planned Bank Robbery we don't approve of unauthorized withdrawals. But we do want to offer—free of charge—bullet-proof vests, ski masks, and, if necessary, a getaway car. This is the compassionate thing to do!

And young people who need some extra cash from their local 7-Eleven shouldn't have to get their parents' permission to obtain this protection. If that were the case, hundreds more teens would be needlessly injured by narrow-minded parents who are trying to inflict their morality on their children.

Again, let me emphasize that Planned Bank Robbery does not condone or encourage grand larceny. We only want to stress it is a personal decision. We're "pro-choice"!

ANECDOTES, STORIES, AND ILLUSTRATIONS

As mentioned in chapter 9, we must put flesh on facts for them to be effective. Clothe arguments in anecdotes, statistics in stories, and ideas in illustrations. Jesus is the best example with His vivid and memorable parables.

HARD, HARD WORK

Finally, writing is just plain hard work. I rejected 99 percent of the manuscripts that came into the office while I served as editorial director with Wesleyan Publishing. The number one reason was that, somehow, the author believed that divine inspiration was sufficient without human perspiration.

For instance, here are a few of my favorite cover letters:

Dear Editor,
God dictated this article to me. I don't even know what it says.
[Fort Wayne, Indiana]

Dear Editor,
GOD told me to write this poem, but your publishing house rejected it. You rejected GOD's poem just before the tornadoes wiped out half your building in 1965. GOD is giving you a second chance to repent and publish my poem. GOD is giving you six weeks.   [Marion, Indiana]

Dear Editor,
God told me to write this article. At least I think it was God. Maybe it was. Maybe it wasn't. Maybe it was the devil.

I don't know. You're an editor. Can you tell me if God wrote
it or the devil?   [Chino, California]

James Kennedy related the story of a woman who came to him
with a poem proclaiming that "the Holy Spirit gave it to me." After
reading the poem, Kennedy said that to accuse the Holy Spirit of a
poem like that was not fair to God.

I *do* believe that God *does* inspire writing:

> But it was to us that God revealed these things by his Spirit.
> For his Spirit searches out everything and shows us God's
> deep secrets. And we have received God's Spirit (not the
> world's spirit), so we can know the wonderful things God has
> freely given us. When we tell you these things, we do not use
> words that come from human wisdom. Instead, we speak
> words given to us by the Spirit, using the Spirit's words to
> explain spiritual truths. (1 Cor. 2:10, 12–13 NLT)

But, no matter how inspired we may feel our writing may be,
remember that the actual writing is our feeble, human effort. God told
me to tell you that. (Just kidding!)

That's why I suggest you get a copy of this publisher's book
Writers on Writing. Jerry B. Jenkins, Liz Curtis Higgs, James Scott
Bell, Karen Ball, Dennis E. Hensley, and many more Christian
authors detail the human perspiration that goes into making God's
inspiration publishable.

RESPECT VS. READERS

One caution: If you want respect, write a book; if you want readers, write an article. It constantly amazes me that people are far more
impressed that I've had thirteen books published than that I've been
published two thousand times in newspapers and magazines.

My best-selling book was certainly not a "best seller" at eleven thousand copies. But that's actually very respectable in book publishing, where ten thousand copies sold is considered very good. In fact, less than 1 percent of published books sell over one hundred thousand copies. (Jerry Jenkins and Max Lucado are extreme exceptions!)

But, my newspaper and magazines articles have reached literally millions of readers, and on my Web site, I have more than one million hits each year. Admittedly, those numbers have not earned me fame or fortune, but they have elicited emails like this one I recently received:

> Your article [on suicide] saved my life tonight and showed me a path toward hope. I have very little words to say, still in severe pain from the death of my boyfriend six months ago. But I felt a need to say thank you.   [Name withheld]

That's better than fame and fortune! And remember, Apollos, who was apparently much more persuasive than the apostle Paul, never put pen to papyrus. Paul is still persuasive today— because he wrote! Apollos is a Bible trivia answer.

From a wise mind comes wise speech; the words of the wise are persuasive.
Proverbs 16:23 NLT

14
CHANGING LIVES THROUGH . . . DELIBERATING

A fter serving on church boards for over thirty years, I've learned a few things:

Flat roofs always leak—but never over the baptistery.

Don't plan a "Seal the Parking Lot" workday on Saturday unless you want a "Clean the Carpet" day on Monday.

The furnace breaks down only on weekends—in January.

Agendas that look the shortest take the longest time.

Committees choose beige.

But the greatest of these is this: boards don't like surprises.

My first experience with the no-surprises rule of church politics occurred when I was leading my first youth group. We had planned an outdoor concert on the front lawn of the church. Unfortunately, we hadn't told the board that "Amazing Grace" and "What a Friend We Have in Jesus" weren't in the band's repertoire. Instead, the huge speakers blasted Christian rock music into the next zip code.

Suddenly a board member appeared and made a determined run for the electrical outlets. He was intercepted by an understanding pastor. I'm not exactly sure what was said, but the plug wasn't pulled, and afterward about fifty teens indicated they wanted to follow Christ.

That was thirty years ago, and people still talk about "that rock concert on the front lawn." It is a lesson I vividly remember.

I've learned that to get new ideas accepted, one needs to be as "shrewd as a snake and harmless as a dove." This doesn't mean to be manipulative or unethical, but there are some prudent ways to institute new ministries or programs. Here's what needs to be done before you present a new proposal to the board.

RUN A SOUND CHECK

I've found it helpful to ask myself some questions—and come up with solid answers—before I recommend an idea. This process helps me present a persuasive case.

Is the Idea Spiritually and Doctrinally Sound?

While our denomination's book of rules and regulations may never be canonized as the inspired Word of God, we do need to respect the doctrines and policies of the church with which we have chosen to associate. So, while "Bingo Night" might lead to an exciting senior citizens' ministry, in the churches I've been involved with, the stand on gambling would guarantee a "no" vote—for the idea and perhaps for you in the next election of church officers.

Is the Idea Well Researched, the Implications Thought Through?

One board member thought it would be great to have farmers donate hogs for a charity luau. After the "yeas" died down, committees were assigned to turn the fellowship hall into a tropical paradise, to publicize the event, to sell tickets, and even to dig a pit in the back lawn—until the health department sent a rather stern letter to the pastor noting that local health codes prohibited such an event. (Now what do we do with five six-hundred-pound hogs?!)

Is the Idea in Good Taste?

One of the highlights of a youth ministry I worked with several years ago was the annual October haunted house. Our director and his staff went all out to provide enough theatrical blood and guts to make even Stephen King squeamish. Then one year, October passed without a mention of "Scream in the Dark." The organization's leaders had decided that mutilated, decapitated bodies were not the best publicity for a Christian organization. Over the years the idea had attracted huge crowds, but perhaps at the expense of good taste.

Is the Idea Ethical?

A friend of mine ran a local teen "night club." Every Saturday night he had music groups perform. I suggested to him the name of a great group—I just didn't mention that it was a Christian group that specialized in concerts for secular crowds. My entire youth board was thrilled with the idea and promised to bring all their friends. No mention was made in the publicity on the local rock station that this was a Christian group.

Sure enough, more than five hundred teens jammed the small club—until they found out it was a Christian group. Within thirty minutes, all that was left was this red-faced youth leader and his youth group. A great idea, but it may have been deceptive—or at least not totally honest.

Will the Idea Have Wide-based Support?

Every youth group I have ever worked with inevitably asks to have a dance, "with Christian music, of course." While there is nothing in our church's written policies to forbid it, most of our members are not open to it. A Christian rock concert on the front lawn, maybe, but not a dance.

In other churches, the issue might be rummage sales, Las Vegas nights, or selling pizzas door to door. When considering such ideas, we have to weigh whether the idea would be harmful to the unity of our church.

RESEARCH THE MARKET

Once we're convinced the idea is spiritually, doctrinally, legally, ethically, and socially sound, we can move to the next step: establishing the need.

As mentioned in chapter 2, nearly half of most advertising campaign costs are for market research. Before we can sell our idea, we need to know the felt needs of the members of our board: Is evangelism a high priority? Is discipleship the focus of the church's ministry? Or is fellowship the main thrust?

If you can show how your idea will meet the perceived needs of the board, you'll have more "yeas" than "nays" when it comes time to vote.

At times, there may be programs that need to be developed, but the board isn't aware—or chooses not to be aware—of the need. In that case, we must document the need.

Such was the case with my proposal for a sex education program at another church where I was assistant pastor. Several parents had spoken to me about their discomfort in discussing sexuality with their young people and felt that the youth group would be the ideal forum. From this informal sample group, I contacted other parents and mentioned the possibility. They also said they'd appreciate this type of program. Armed with their backing, the need was well established, but I still wasn't ready to go to the board.

I knew I needed to anticipate and answer objections before they could be voiced. I knew that the unspoken assumptions of many would be "Sex education has no place in church!"; "The church should stick to preaching the gospel"; "We never had sex education when I was a kid, and I turned out OK!"; "Talking about sex will make kids want to experiment with it!"; "I'm not comfortable talking about the subject"; "There's no one to teach it."

I worked through each objection and tried to answer each fairly and honestly.

TEST, TEST, TEST

Testing of a program is vital before gearing up for full-scale production.

Talk to the pastor and board members individually about your idea. Make it as casual as possible. You're not selling vacuum cleaners, so don't make it a hard sell. Think of it as sowing seeds that, at the next meeting, may begin to germinate.

In some cases, another board member will "steal" your idea and present it to the board. I'm happy when that happens. I often intentionally sow idea seeds hoping they'll germinate and someone else will develop them to maturity. I have a lot more ideas than I have time to develop fully.

Probably the number one reason that ideas don't receive a positive response is that there has not been sufficient preparation before the idea is put on the table. Until you sense that the pastor or the majority of the board is behind it, keep working the previous steps.

WRAP THE PACKAGE

Finally, in making a more formal presentation, packaging is a key element.

Collect materials needed for the idea. In my case, I went to the local Christian bookstore and cleaned out their section on love and sexuality. I told the manager that I was collecting proposed study materials and asked to take them out for review. She was happy to let me have them free for two weeks.

Establish objectives and format. From the stacks of books, I developed a list of specific objectives for the sex education course.

As illustration, here were my three objectives:

1. To provide sound medical information on sexual development at appropriate age levels.

2. To provide biblical principles relating to sexual behavior at appropriate age levels.

3. To help parents provide their children with a healthy appreciation for their sexual makeup, and to assist their children in making biblical choices in sexual behavior.

I also determined the format—six meetings after evening church services for both parents and young people.

Now that I had some definite objectives, and had planned for the objections, I was ready for the next step.

DON'T EXPECT YOUR IDEA TO GO UNCHALLENGED OR UNAMMENDED

It has taken nearly thirty years, but I am gradually becoming less intimidated by objections, "concerns," or bad votes concerning my ideas. A thick skin is a necessary attribute, but so is the ability to recognize a valid criticism and adjust your proposal along the way.

Because of the feedback I got, the sex education proposal promptly went from six meetings to one, and from a meeting with parents and young people to a meeting with just parents.

But through the meeting, parents did receive some practical tools to open up the discussion with their children about love and sex.

And since that meeting went well, the next year the young people were invited.

So, if you're planning an outdoor Christian rock concert on the church's front lawn, please be persuasive by prayer, planning, and preparation. And guard the electrical outlets!

"I'm here [with] an invitation to a changed life, changed inside and out."
Jesus, Luke 5:31 MSG

AFTERWORD

A s I mentioned in the very first chapter, my goals for this book are that (a) you will learn biblical and psychological principles for writing and speaking to change lives, (b) you will feel inspired to write material and speak in a way that will actually change lives, and (c) you will write material and speak in a way that will actually change lives. There is nothing more satisfying and fulfilling!

I'm sure, however, I've left something important out of this book, so please visit www.jameswatkins.com/communicate/htm for updates and expanded material.

And if you found this book helpful, please (a) let me know by emailing me at jim@jameswatkins.com, (b) tell your friends (or better yet, buy copies for all your friends), (c) write a glowing review at amazon.com, and (d) invite me to teach these principles to your group or organization. Thanks!

Jim

OTHER BOOKS BY JAMES WATKINS